Still Believing

FAITH MEETS FAITH

An Orbis Series in Interreligious Dialogue
Paul F. Knitter & William R. Burrows, General Editors
Editorial Advisors
John Berthrong
Diana Eck
Karl-Josef Kuschel
Lamin Sanneh
George E. Tinker
Felix Wilfred

In the contemporary world, the many religions and spiritualities stand in need of greater communication and cooperation. More than ever before, they must speak to, learn from, and work with each other in order to maintain their vital identities and to contribute to fashioning a better world.

The FAITH MEETS FAITH Series seeks to promote interreligious dialogue by providing an open forum for exchange among followers of different religious paths. While the Series wants to encourage creative and bold responses to questions arising from contemporary appreciations of religious plurality, it also recognizes the multiplicity of basic perspectives concerning the methods and content of interreligious dialogue.

Although rooted in a Christian theological perspective, the Series does not limit itself to endorsing any single school of thought or approach. By making available to both the scholarly community and the general public works that represent a variety of religious and methodological viewpoints, FAITH MEETS FAITH seeks to foster an encounter among followers of the religions of the world on matters of common concern.

FAITH MEETS FAITH SERIES

Still Believing

Jewish, Christian, and Muslim Women Affirm Their Faith

Edited by
Victoria Lee Erickson
Susan A. Farrell

ORBIS BOOKS

Maryknoll, New York 10545

Founded in 1970, Orbis Books endeavors to publish works that enlighten the mind, nourish the spirit, and challenge the conscience. The publishing arm of the Maryknoll Fathers and Brothers, Orbis seeks to explore the global dimensions of the Christian faith and mission, to invite dialogue with diverse cultures and religious traditions, and to serve the cause of reconciliation and peace. The books published reflect the opinions of their authors and are not meant to represent the official position of the Maryknoll Society. To obtain more information about Maryknoll and Orbis Books, please visit our website at www.maryknoll.org.

Library of Congress Cataloging-in-Publication Data

Still believing : Jewish, Christian, and Muslim women affirm their faith /
Victoria Lee Erickson, Susan A. Farrell, editors.
    p. cm. — (Faith meets faith)
  ISBN 1-57075-582-5 (pbk.)
  1. Muslim women—Religious life. 2. Christian women—Religious life.
3. Jewish women—Religious life. I. Erickson, Victoria Lee, 1955– II.
Farrell, Susan A. III. Series.
  BL625.7.S75 2005
  200'.82—dc22
                              2004027710

Contents

PART III
OPENING THE ANCIENT TREASURE BOX OF FAITH

Contributors

Nurah W. Ammat'ullah (Rosalie P. Jeter), MLIS, GC, Executive Director of The Muslim Women's Institute for Research and Development, is a program developer who focuses on faith-based community development initiatives. Over the years her programs have been aimed at building capacity among poor and immigrant communities in the Bronx. Clients served by the programs are predominantly immigrants with transitional needs that are culturally specific. She is involved in a number of multifaith and NGO organizations, including Women in Religious Leadership, Women in Islam, Interfaith Spiritual Caregivers, and Auburn Theological Seminary's Women's Multifaith Planning Committee.

Kathleen Duffy, a Sister of Saint Joseph, is Professor of Physics at Chestnut Hill College. In the past Kathleen has also taught physics at Drexel University, Bryn Mawr College, Ateneo de Manila University, and University of the Philippines. She has published articles in atomic and molecular physics and nonlinear dynamics in the *Journal of Chemical Physics*, *Journal of Physical Chemistry*, *Journal de Physique*, *Physical Review Letters*, as well as Philippine journals and bulletins. Her present research focuses on the work and synthetic methods of the Jesuit paleontologist Pierre Teilhard de Chardin. She has published work in this area in *Teilhard Studies*. Kathleen is involved in the emerging science and religion dialogue. She has received a John Templeton Foundation Science and Religion course award as well as the Quality and Excellence in Teaching award from the Center for Theology and the Natural Sciences. She has organized programs and lectures at Chestnut Hill College to support ongoing interest in these topics. She also serves on the Board of Directors of the Metanexus Institute for Religion and Science and the American Teilhard Association. In keeping with a long-term interest in the work of Teilhard de Chardin and Thomas Berry, she has developed a multimedia narrative of the Universe Story and uses it as a basis for guided retreats and presentations.

Victoria Lee Erickson, an independent researcher, was most recently the Chaplain and Associate Professor of the Sociology of Religion, Drew University. A Christian practitioner, she has served the academy on several levels including The American Sociological Association as elected Religion Section member. Her publications include *Where Silence Speaks: Feminism,*

Social Theory and Religion (Fortress Press); *Surviving Terror: Hope and Justice in a World of Violence*, edited with Michelle Lim Jones (Brazos Press); and "Georg Simmel: American Sociology Chooses *The Stone the Builders Refused*," in *The Blackwell Reader in the Sociology of Religion*, edited by Richard Fenn (Blackwell).

Susan A. Farrell, Professor of Sociology, Kingsborough Community College, CUNY, is a Roman Catholic laywoman and longstanding board member of Catholics for a Free Choice. She has served the academy as the managing editor of *Gender & Society* for Sociologists for Women in Society and as an elected member of various committees in the American Sociological Society, the Eastern Sociological Association, and Sociologists for Women and Society. She reviews for many journals. Her publications include *The Power of Gender in Religion*, with Georgie Ann Weatherby (McGraw-Hill); *Social Construction of Gender*, with Judith Lorber (Sage); *Families and the Life Cycle: Integrating Macro and Mirco Systems*, with Marvin Shapiro (McGraw-Hill); and *The Essential Sociologist*, with Beth Hess and Peter Stein (Roxbury).

Rhonda Hustedt Jacobsen, Assistant Dean for Faculty Development and Professor of Psychology, Messiah College, is a member of the United Church of Christ and a professional within church-related higher education. Her scholarship merges the faith world of beliefs, practices, and affections with the analytic, strategic, and empathic modes of scholarship. A recipient of several teaching awards, including the Sears Roebuck Teaching Excellence and Campus Leadership Award, she has also received a number of grants from the John Templeton Foundation for her work in the area of science and religion. Her publications include *Scholarship and Christian Faith*, with Douglas Jacobsen, forthcoming (Oxford University Press).

Azza M. Karam, Director, Women's Program World Conference on Religion and Peace, the United Nations, is an Egyptian Muslim. Her publications include *Islamisms and the State* (Macmillan); *Women in Parliament: Beyond Numbers* (International IDEA); and *Transnational Political Islam*, forthcoming (Pluto). She serves on many boards, including the Board of the International Dialogue's Foundation in The Hague; the Board of Directors of the Association of Women in Development in Washington; and the Euromediterranean Charter of Peace and Change at the Bruno Kreisky Foundation for International Dialogue in Vienna.

Anna Karpathakis, Assistant Professor of Behavioral Sciences at Kingsborough Community College, CUNY, is a member of the Greek Orthodox Church of North America. She has served on the Editorial Board of *Teaching Sociology*, a publication of the American Sociological Association. She has lectured widely in the areas of globalization, diaspora identities, ethnicity, immigration, and women's issues. Her publications include *New York Glory: Religions in the City* (NYU); and "Greek Immigrants, the Family and Assimilation: A Sociologically Informed Autobiography," in *Dominant-Minority Relations*, edited by J. P. Myers, forthcoming (Allyn & Bacon).

Judith Lorber, Professor Emerita of Brooklyn College, CUNY, is the founding editor of *Gender & Society* and has served on many editorial boards. She was elected President of the Eastern Sociological Society and the Sociologists for Women in Society, and Vice President for the Study of Social Problems. Her publications include *Gender and the Social Construction of Illness* (Altamira); *Paradoxes of Gender* (Yale); *Women Physicians: Careers, Status, and Power* (Tavistock); and *Breaking the Bowls: Gender Theory and Feminist Change*, forthcoming (Norton). She is Jewish and widely supportive of women's communities of nurture.

Mira Morgenstern, Assistant Professor of Political Science, Kingsborough Community College, CUNY, identifies with the Orthodox Jewish community. Her publications include *Rousseau and the Politics of Ambiguity: Self, Culture, and Society* (Pennsylvania State University Press); "A Life Cycle in Code," in *Jewish Mothers Tell Their Stories,* edited by Rachel Siegel, Ellen Cole, and Susan Steinberg-Oren (Haworth); "Amour de soi, amour-propre, et formation du citoyen," in *Politique et Nation*, edited by Robert Thiéry (Champion); and "Women and the Politics of Ambiguity," in *Feminist Reinterpretations of Rousseau*, forthcoming (Pennsylvania State University Press). A community practitioner, she connects academic resources and everyday problems, for example, "Self and Other in Rousseau," in *Essays on the Modern Identity*, edited by William D. Brewer and Carole Lambert (Peter Lang); and "Ruth and the Sense of Self," in *Judaism* (Spring 1999).

Vanessa L. Ochs is Associate Professor of Jewish Studies and Ida and Nathan Kolodiz Director of Jewish Studies at the University of Virginia. Her publications include *New Jewish Ritual,* forthcoming (Jewish Publications Society); *The Book of Sacred Jewish Practices*, edited with Irwin Kula (Jewish Lights); "The Contemporary Hagaddah" and "Rituals of Mourning," in *Religious Practices in America*, edited by Colleen McDannell (Princeton); "Women and Ritual Artifacts," in *Women of the Wall*, edited by Phyllis Chesler and Rivka Haut (Jewish Lights); *Words on Fire: One Woman's Journey into the Sacred* (Westview); and *Safe and Sound* (Penguin). A recipient of a fellowship from the National Endowment for the Arts, Ochs is the editor of the Sacred Day series of CLAL, the National Jewish Center for Learning and Leadership.

Dina Pinsky, Assistant Professor of Sociology at Arcadia University, has extensive experience researching Jewish life, with an emphasis on American Jewish identity. She is writing a book based on her interview study of second-wave Jewish feminists. Her most recent work has focused on constructions of Jewish masculinity.

Louise M. Temple is head of the Biology Department, James Madison University. She actively includes undergraduate scholars in her research projects, which include ongoing studies in immunology, toxicology, and pharmacology. She reviews for USDA, NSF, and McGraw-Hill. Her publications include "Carbohydrate Catabolism of *Pseudomonas aeruginosa*," with A. Sages and P. V. Phibbs Jr., in *Biotechnology Handbooks: Pseudomonas,* edited by T. Montie (Plenum Press); "ELISA to Measure SRBC-Specific IgM: Method and Data Evaluation," with L. Butterworth, T. T. Kawabata, A. E. Munson, and K. L. White Jr., in *Modern Methods in Immunotoxicology*, edited by G. R. Burleson, J. H. Dean, and A. E. Munson (Wiley-Liss).

Introduction

What Believers Know

VICTORIA LEE ERICKSON
with SUSAN A. FARRELL

Believers know that while our values
are embodied in tradition,
our hopes are always located in change.
—William Sloan Coffin

This book contains a collection of personal stories about "believing and having faith through the years," told by women academics and community professionals who are Muslims, Christians, and Jews.* These scholarly women, for many reasons, remain connected to faith traditions and communities while participating in a wide range of faith practices. These stories tell how their faith perspectives structure their lives and how the structure of their lives is affected by "believing," by "having faith," and by "belonging." A scholarly/professional analysis of "why I believe after all these years" assumes that faith, believing, and belonging are challenged over the years and

---

* We are grateful to a colleague for alerting us to Rochelle Garner's well-researched and well-written book *Contesting the Terrain of the Ivory Tower: Spiritual Leadership of African-American Women in the Academy* (New York: Routledge, 2004). As our book goes to press, we decided to include mention of Garner's historical and contemporary cultural study of African American women deans who possess spiritually based education leadership agendas. These women's stories share commitments to spiritually guided leadership through servanthood, an ethic of care, attention to social justice, and to taking all of this beyond the borders of the academy to produce, in the spirit of Mary McLeod Bethune, hope, love, confidence, respect, dignity, harmony, ambition, responsibility, and courage to change. Please read this book as a sisterly companion of the great journey to transform one of society's most important social institutions.

that one's continued commitments are reflections of decisions to remain "faithful, believing, and/or connected."

The well-documented conflict in the academy over the expressed faith commitments of its scientists is one such challenge to the public practice of faith. To what extent do women of faith live these commitments in public? What impact does the public nature of faith, as it is played out in the professional worlds, have on the changes these authors wish to see made in an imperfect and hurting world? What insights into the complexities of faith and its practices do these academic women of the Abrahamic traditions offer a world searching for peace—especially when it is a search for peace among members of the Abrahamic traditions?

These are a few questions seeking responses that flow through these pages. And that is how we hope you read this book: like a river flowing. We know where we are in a river by the ever-changing markers on its banks. The purpose of the academy is to produce recognizable markers—guides and warning signs—that help us encounter the new moment as we travel unknown and known ways.

It is possible to know today what we have sought to know for so long. Such is the sentiment of our authors, who have been given the great gift of a university education and who seek to know the whole universe as we offer to our collective understanding specialized knowledge produced in our disciplines. Interfaith and interdisciplinary encounters require deep listening. As Michel de Certeau has taught us, when we listen to voices we have not heard before something changes inside of us. When we listen to others we discover not only them, but ourselves. In *The Capture of Speech* he writes:

> Voices that had never been heard began to change us. At least that was what we felt. From this something unheard of was produced: we began to speak. It seemed as if it were for the first time. From everywhere emerged the treasures, either aslumber or tacit, of forever unspoken experiences. (De Certeau 1997, 11–12)

This emergence de Certeau calls a kind of "festival" in which "something happened to us . . . emerging from who knows where." There are delightful moments in this book when voices come to us "from who knows where." This book is very much like a festival, a smorgasbord of ideas, experiences, visions, and hopes. Yet, there is a commonness, a red thread if you will, running through the pages. It is simply this: acting with knowledge gained from *the holy other* brings personal and communal wholeness.

The Abrahamic traditions have always sought to gather knowledge from across the world. Our authors are world travelers, experienced in the documentary tasks necessary to bring the distant stories of others into a sound and focused hearing in the local context that then produces life-giving attitudes and appropriate judgments. All but one author holds a doctorate (and this one is planning on finishing hers soon). Scientists and practitioners in their own right, our authors have provided us with insights into faith and belief gathered from their own special places in the world. What is exceptional about this book is that these scientists are speaking—there is much pressure in the academic world not to speak about one's faith and belief—and greater pressure still not to set faith narratives into a theoretical context that might point out a universal and authoritative word. Indeed, there is more than pressure, there are often negative consequences for academics who dare to speak about "pure belief." Those that speak here have obviously agreed to tell their stories.

THE SOUL'S STORY

"Through story telling, the community of souls narrates a world. The soul's story is archived in liturgies and festivals that anchor memory. Georg Simmel called that space bounded by the activity of the soul, *society*" (Erickson 2001). Simmel, a founding member of the German Sociological Association, believed that society is the product of humans working to be the best they can be, that is, humans moving toward the goal of salvation. Human relationships, then, are all religious ones as we seek to create bridges between each other. Simmel believed that when humans seek to be like God, they create what theology calls hope, and what he as a sociologist called *sociability*. Sociability is a way of relating in which each person seeks the well-being of the other. The classical sociologists understood that society is only possible through the power of believing that connection with others is possible, that we can know and be known by others.

The model many humans use to create connections with others and to know and to be known by others is their relationship with God. Through human and divine relationships religion creates the world it envisions. Religion is a human institution—like education, banking, the media, government, and the like. Many people believe that religion is the source institution from which these other institutions were born. It is important, then, to remember that just as many people believe that the soul is the well that religion dips into for its power. The soul, the original gift from God, is bigger and more powerful than the institutions it creates.

The soul's story is multi-vocal. The soul tells the story of religion (its encounter with other souls) as it is transcending religion itself and as it is telling the bigger story of the soul's encounter with God, the Holy One, who is not held captive by religion or the soul. When many souls tell of our encounters with God, we discover that we all belong to the Holy One, that we are brothers and sisters, kinfolk, in a new territory where our lives blend together with our Source. This story is a collective one; it belongs to you and to me.

A READING OF OUR AUTHORS'
COLLECTIVE UNDERSTANDING OF FAITH

When we gather our authors' understandings of faith and add these understandings together, we discover that we have a larger concept than any one story is able to tell by itself. This integrated summary will help us understand the particular faith communities from which these understandings come.

Above all, faith creates life, empowered agency, and it is the source of life that we give to others. This life we often locate "in the heart," but it is also "of the mind." Faith that integrates the whole being creates a "oneness" of great magnitude. This oneness is expressed through a variety of communicative forms, most notably music and art. Faith seeks communication with society. As it engages society through its many languages, faith traditions establish an operating program, a way to belong to others. This way of belonging to others is what we call *identity*. Our identity is a sum statement of our desire for a shared life with others, for community. Faith as a foundation for identity, then, is a wonder-filled happening—how does it come to be that we create a home in this world with each other, even those we do not know, those without faces? Given the difficulty of establishing faith, many of us see it as a "struggle" with culture that in the best of all worlds turns into a "conversation" with culture. This conversation seemingly makes us vulnerable, and we warn each other against being coopted. We say things like: "build your house upon the rock." We have discovered that if we stand up and remain who we are in the culture conversations, we are more likely to be the source of peace and social justice that comes through and from our faith histories and traditions.

In this multifaith world, our authors are clear about several things. First, our religious power to act must be tempered by education. The Abrahamic traditions are clear about the need for an educated mind of faith. This education expands our creativity so that we may come together as a diverse people and build a world that houses our hopes and dreams. That is why we are in the academy. We feel called by the Divine to be an educative resource linking our students and our colleagues to a better future. Our faith rightly calls us to be as good as we can be, offering back our created selves to the Creator.

It is easier for some of our authors to think about God than it is about the faith community itself—of which they say they belong, belong not so well, or belong not at all. Our authors are all aware of the need to belong but have justifiably pointed to the human failings that keep people from belonging. Even so, most authors find that belonging to a faith community that is dedicated to improving the lives of its members and the world, even in the midst of uncertainty and struggle, brings great reward found in spiritual and other life satisfactions.

FAITH COMMUNITIES

Our pursuit of a deeper understanding of the whys and hows of believing and belonging leads us into the sticky conversation regarding social systems and culture (for an interesting treatment of the subject, see Hays 1994). Whereas culture is often seen as a meaning-making system, separate and different from social systems, Hays puts the package of ideas together in a different way, demonstrating that culture is itself the combination of systems of relations and systems of meaning. What connects them is what they exchange: power. Both relational systems and systems of meaning are materially and symbolically matched in durability and transcendent nature while they remain analytically distinct. This understanding of culture allows us to read religion as a culture and to talk about religious cultures. Religion is both a system set of social relations with patterns, roles, relationships, and forms of domination and a system of meaning containing beliefs, values, special languages, forms of knowledge, material artifacts, and practices that shape a way of life. In this book we understand the people who produce both the social relations and attendant meaning-making practices to be members of a faith community. Membership in the faith community moves along on a sliding scale of believing and belonging.

Although all religions accept converts, our membership in faith communities tends to be seen publicly as either by *right of birth*, as in tribal communities such as Judaism and African traditional religions and indigenous peoples, or *by confession,* as we see in Christianity, Islam, and Buddhism. Membership is an anthropologically complicated reality in all religions, where practices must be examined for meaning in their own right. In both kinds of communities holy languages create global communication networks that assist the religious mind in understanding itself as not bounded by geography, even if it holds dear particular religious landscapes. Through language, religion provides members with resources to fulfill their obligations to God and God's created order. This originating "heart and soul" language seeks its counterpart wherever it goes.

Membership in a faith community is determined by each member's sense of a moral imperative to protect. The act of protection is a matter of conscience shaped by an original faith community that instilled in each member principles of "right and wrong." Members of faith communities do not necessarily share beliefs, rites, or practices. Their commonality is based on a desire for a interactive relationship demanded by conscience (Erickson 2003).

Membership practices such as worship, singing, dancing, reading, studying, praying, teaching, storytelling, punishment and correction, mediation, and life-cycle rituals are ways through which members inherit values, culture, and wisdom from their faith communities. Worship is perhaps the most critical practice of the faith community. Through worship, communities summarize their histories, establishing understandings of the present moment and the future to come. Through worship people come to know who they are and who they want to become. The faithful created the first intellectual home for what we now call science and established sanctuaries for free thought. However, the history of faith communities also carries with it distressing and regrettable periods of persecution and violence against competing world views and their leaders.

These distressing moments are often linked to what sociologists call "the definition of the situation." How we read the context and each other, often in a split second, shapes how we respond. How we act is an actualization of our moral character (Haan et al. 1985). Our character may or may not be of sufficient quality to transcend social situations. We are continually walking into situations that require us to process information, seek information, create information, and then produce deliberate rational acts (Ball-Rokeach 1973). In the global context the faith community's religious education is often the only reservoir out of which we draw the resources for character building and the character's action. This reservoir is continually fed by our personal experiences and our many kinds of teachers and coaches. Religious and moral teachers over time add biblical and theological reflection, commentaries, sermons, and the like that update the listening communities' understanding of themselves, the world around them, and the relational responsibilities they have to themselves and to others.

It is important, then, to teach the young to live with a certain amount of ambiguity, which is itself the raft that helps us over the temporarily "unbridged" rivers of life. Tolerating moments of uncertainty and ambiguity and using them to produce knowledge requires rethinking most of what we have come to assume. What makes reeducation complicated is that the mechanisms for the production of character and knowledge are taught to children by age four, firmly established by ages eight to ten, and tested at ritual events like confirmation and bar/bat mitzvah around ages thirteen to sixteen. The knowledge produced by this instruction is hoped to produce a fully functioning adult who becomes a model citizen in community and society. The greatest source of knowledge for adults in faith communities continues to be interaction with the holy books of their traditions; the lives of their saints, heroes, heroines, and prophets; and the experience of the people invested in memories and liturgies. A good, rightly acting adult is produced, or not, in childhood. After the family produces a moral actor, our social institutions pick up the task and continue the educating and reeducating process as a normal course of events by offering educational programs, media events that give information, and the like. In this way society continues the process of producing leaders.

A significant task of religious leaders is facilitating the healing of body and soul. Healing is an educative process that mends the broken physical and social body. The mending of the social body is often called peace-making. Individual and society bodies are restored in order to return them to faithful living.

SOCIETY IS FAITHFULNESS

Through the isolation and chaos of his life caused by anti-Semitism and his own resisting of the harmonization of the disciplinary voice, Simmel observed that faithfulness between institutions and citizens is much like faithfulness between spouses. Through faithfulness we come to love each other. Love built on faithfulness is *love without reservation* (Simmel 1950, 328). It is this love that society needs in order to connect us "one to the other," whether in corporations, churches, schools, hospitals, or neighborhoods. Love-based connectedness preserves the self, the couple, the unit, the society. Love-based connection creates societal familihood where no one is *the stranger*. Love creates the embraced, included object.

When society is in chaos, as it always is, faithfulness rises above the fragmentation and builds footings on whatever ground it touches, making possible the bridging work of humans (Erickson 1999). Ernst Troeltsch, Simmel's colleague, argued that a country dependent on a citizenry that does not feel responsible for the well-being of the other, that does not feel responsible for creating form and bridging the fragments, totters on the brink of disaster (Starr 1996). Simmel writes:

> Practical faith is the fundamental quality of the soul that in essence is sociological, that is, it becomes concretized as a relationship with some being external to the self. . . . The purely social significance of this religious faith beyond that of the individual faith has not yet been investigated at all, but I feel sure that without it, society as we know it would not exist. Our capacity to have faith in a person or a group of people beyond all demonstrable evidence to the contrary—is one of the most stable bonds holding society together. (Simmel 1997, 169–70)

THE FAITH COMMUNITY'S STORYTELLING FAITH

In this book we present faith narratives of women who speak simply and directly about their experiences with believing. It would be true to say of the editors that one reason we collected these stories is that our life work has centered around understanding and validating faith narratives that authentically seek to live the peace and well-being of their respective faith traditions. This validation process does not invalidate our own narratives but, perhaps surprisingly to some readers, reinforces their powerfulness. The purpose of intra-faith and interfaith storytelling is not the trouncing of one story by another, but the pure encounter of the other and the engagement of values, commitments, and visions. In all of their diversity, human stories share a structure that is embedded in language and language formation. For a contemporary and nondoctrinal navigating of the story world we recommend

Michael Roemer's *Telling Stories* (1995). To help us read these stories we would like to lift out a few of Roemer's key points:

1. The story is always about something in the past. We cannot predict how the reader/listener will respond to it; the reader is accountable for the response, which is both to the story and to the self. The story combined with its response is itself a kind of truth-telling.

2. To produce this truth in us, the story encourages us to forget what we know momentarily so that the story can tell us what it knows. In the story we are free to listen, but we are also vulnerable because we have opened ourselves up to the truth in the story—the reality beyond the text itself and beyond our own stories.

3. The story can't tell everything, so it chooses what to tell; the hearer must "temporarily surrender" to the storyteller's art. In so doing, we create a shared but "temporary community" with the characters in the story. This experience is one of "democracy" wherein everyone is authentically heard.

We hope you, the reader, will encounter these stories—which are now history as the authors have gone on to live, change, and grow—with a sense of openness and gratefulness for the gift the author is to our human community. If their stories create a story drama in your life, well, this is as story should be. The transfer of dramatization into the current moment represents the success of the storyteller, who has become a human resource to your own self-understanding.

Storytellers are important anchors in the narrative production of life. In university life the generations tell the story differently as the disciplines expand their knowledge bases. Randall Collins notes that we experience the disappearance of intellectual generations much like all experiences of mortality: "More than ever, it seems now that we are left without giants among us, and must make do for ourselves" (1986). It is difficult enough for academics to experience generational stability, much less, as Collins points out, what the Bible and antiquity referred to as a time of "ripeness and fulfillment, a time when honor is given to wisdom accumulated over the years." For several of the women writing in this book, the absence of women "giants" in both their religious and scientific lives left them painfully aware of the history of gender exclusion and the absence of both honor and presence. For women looking exclusively for women role models, life can be lonely indeed. Whether for good or bad theoretical and practical reasons, excluding men and including only women in one's intellectual generational pool severely limits access to any accumulated wisdom that might exist. Most of our authors decided to be inclusive and, as Collins notes that Erving Goffman did, live "across several intellectual generations . . . creating a leading position . . . in each one . . . a sign of greatness" (Collins 1986, 107). What is true about the giants and founders of sociology is that they drew on insights from philosophy, theology, history, and economics as they sought to put their intimate knowledge of religion, and the impact of faith in the social world, into play.

FAITHFULLY ANTICIPATING THE ANSWER: THE WORD IN PLAY

Mikhail Mikhalovich Bakhtin (1865–1975), a leading twentieth-century Russian scholar, sought to preserve dialogue through an academic understanding of its structure and use. For Bakhtin, words seek answers in human dialogue. As we write, we anticipate an answer from the listener (Bakhtin 1981). In this book the editors asked the authors to tell us about "still believing after all these years." In the epilogue you will find the editors' response, our "answering word." On another level you, the reader, have an "answering word" to the book's invitation to you to think about the responses these chapters create in you.

As you read you will discover along with Bakhtin that every word is already influenced by the answering word it anticipates. Before I speak, I anticipate your response. Here you find yourself anticipated—we hope we have started a dialogue even though we realize that such a small book cannot in actuality provide a mirror for every reader. Our goal is to point out the possibilities of connection that result from multiple voices in dialogue and to point to the creative lives that have resulted from new conceptual systems that allowed the horizon to break through into new territory.

To start you out on your journey with the authors in this book we present a very brief summary of a journey a word takes from our anticipation of engaging each other in meaningful dialogue to the hoped for conclusion of a new relationship. The word is *Santa Claus*, and the discussion is the role Santa Claus as an "answering word" might play in producing a more serious consciousness of God and science.

Professor Duffy, a Sister of Saint Joseph and physicist, and Professor Temple, an organist and biologist, share a surprising interest in the role of Santa Claus in developing a cosmological consciousness. Both authors have deep spiritualities. Duffy writes on her experience of God and science: "I know a oneness of a greater magnitude. . . . Today, a star-studded sky more easily evokes in me the quietly alluring presence of a personal Creative Power, a God who is large enough to satisfy my soul." Temple writes, "Born into a Christian family with deep historical and personal roots in their faith . . . my spiritual formation has stayed with me for life." Both look back on their long lives of ultimately successful personal struggles to integrate science and religion, and they wish that their experience of Santa Claus had been a different one, one that might have helped them better and still more successfully integrate their lives.

Temple: It was in the mimosa tree one hot July evening that into my consciousness popped the realization that Mama and Daddy were Santa

Claus. I remember crying a little, then going to tell them . . . that I had figured it out. . . . I don't do my thinking in mimosa trees as an adult, but I do re-visit the mimosa tree every year in one of my science classes. It turns out that the leaf of this tree has an unusual characteristic whereby the leaflets all close together when touched. I use this example as a context for describing a very intricate and complex cell signaling mechanism that is well understood in many, but not all aspects. Our scientific knowledge is like this example; we understand so much, but gaps remain—those gaps may be much larger than we currently imagine, but we as curious and inquisitive human beings will continue to search out answers to our scientific questions. When we gain understanding, then will the magic be gone? No more than is the joy of giving and receiving gone when the myth of Santa fades during childhood.

Duffy: When I was a child, I remember asking my mother about Santa Claus, sharing with her my doubts about his existence. I had figured out, I told her, that Santa could not be real because it would be impossible for one person to get around to all those houses on one single night. My mother confirmed my rational assessment. Although on one level I appreciate her honest response, on another, I find it an unfortunate one. This revelation somehow flattened my sense of reality, encouraged my rational approach, and confirmed my suspicion of the nonrational. What if my mother had instead told me yet another story, one that would have led me further into the heart of the Santa Claus myth. Native peoples know this technique. They know how to point to a deeper reality when language fails.

So do the great poets and the mystics. How much better it would have been if my mother had encouraged me to hold the question, to live in and with the mystery. . . . That was not to be. So, here I was again, some years later, doubting my belief in God, another story that seemed too good to be true, but, this time, with no one to confirm my suspicion. Likewise, my cosmic sense, so apparent to me as I remember myself lying on the front lawn, was never developed. A truly integrated person is one who can hold many questions in her heart. Questions about the way Santa travels on Christmas night, questions about the origin of the universe, questions about God, questions about social change, questions about the meaning of life, questions about death . . .

Both scientists wished that the adults in their lives had helped them hold on to the magic of Santa, even as they became aware of the story's truths. The quick adult response to cut off the magic in favor of one kind of truth destroyed yet another kind of truth: that mystery and wonder are the ways the heart and head reconcile themselves. Mystery and wonder are the ways we figure things out. These scientists went on to discover that God and science were equally difficult to believe in, as difficult as Santa. Playfully leaving hope for Santa might have changed the way religion and science unfolded for them both. Religion and science hold many questions and doubts that do not fundamentally change the end result of religious and scientific thinking, which is that both the believer and the scientist must decide to act on what they assume to be true—even if it is disproved tomorrow. This is an act of faith, sometimes of pure belief. In the moment of believing, both the faithful and the scientist live in a moment of poetic creativity that becomes the confident source of the next great moment of insight.

What the children wanted from their parents was a relationship with Santa that would keep their anticipation of surprise and joy alive as they anticipated life now with a new knowledge, with a new kind of "Santa consciousness." The same is true about God, the angels, Elijah. . . . Children anticipate a living, open, real dialogue with the moral agents they encounter, whether seen or unseen. Ideally, by age four children have an intricately developed moral consciousness that, as they age, continually seeks to be a part of the potential of the moral and physical universe. Yes, Elijah will appear at Passover and the angels will bring you good news! How we anticipate a real encounter with moral forces shapes how our relationships develop in the human world and therefore how our conceptual systems, the ways in which we think, are shaped as well.

In the consciousness of the Abrahamic family, a person continually open to the appearance of the miraculous is one open to a new encounter with a human being that is anticipated as a miracle as well. This openness creates a new kind of language that expands the boundaries of our world, giving us new territory in which to encounter the other in a creative and expanded relationship. For a host of reasons, including their own early and deep spiritual development, all of our authors, regardless of their experience with the adults in their world, or their encounters with Santa, Elijah, or the angels, decided to keep anticipating a living conversation with others. You will find in these chapters amazing women creating a responsive and supportive world that seeks conversation with others and, in so doing, producing yet new avenues for listening and building new relationships that help them reach for new horizons in science and religion.

We hope that you enjoy reading these chapters. Each story is very different from the others. Feel free to write in your copy of this book. Agree and disagree with the authors. Make connections among the stories and between your story and these stories. The Epilogue, the last chapter of the book, is where we will meet you again. It is our hope that in the end we will find a new beginning, a new way to appreciate the hard work and sheer fun at play with the educated mind and heart.

PART I

A Legacy of Believing

1

That All May Be One

KATHLEEN DUFFY

As a child lying on our front lawn looking up at the stars, I had no idea how huge and how wonderful the universe really is. Nor did I have any sense of the extent of the inner and outer journeys that would lead me to my present understanding of the cosmos and to my present experience of God. Yet, despite the fact that I was probably only ten years old, I felt a strong and intimate connection to the cosmos without noticing that this experience had anything to do with the pervasive presence of God. It was only later that I came to realize that the stillness of the night, the patterns in the sky that drew me beyond myself, were charged with God. I now know that this early experience of transcendence held the key to my unique journey into God.

A dark, starry night still has power to move my heart. Now, as I peer through my telescope into those star nurseries where huge masses of gas and dust are collapsing into stars, I know a oneness of a greater magnitude. The simple elements that are being drawn into these emerging stellar systems are the same as those that make up our solar system. They contain within them a potential as creative as the ones that produced my body. Today, a star-studded sky more easily evokes in me the quietly alluring presence of a personal Creative Power, a God who is large enough to satisfy my soul.

IN THE BEGINNING

Yet, the journey from that shy little girl lying on the front lawn to a woman who is physicist, Sister of Saint Joseph, and believer was not an easy one. As a child I was taught to read the biblical stories of creation literally. It was not until high school that one of my religion teachers presented an evolutionary view of life and of the cosmos. After some interior struggle, her words convinced me that a God who could create a creative world was much more powerful than one who designed a prefabricated one. I have always been grateful to her for starting me on an evolutionary path.

15

At the time, though, my newfound evolutionary understanding of creation was still quite frail. In the pre–Vatican II Roman Catholic Church, very few held, wrote about, or taught this view. This was unsettling for me, so much so that I began to wonder about the existence of God, even to question God's existence.

When I was a child, I remember asking my mother about Santa Claus, sharing with her my doubts about his existence. I had figured out, I told her, that Santa could not be real because it would be impossible for one person to get around to all those houses on one single night. My mother confirmed my rational assessment. Although on one level I appreciate her honest response, on another, I find it an unfortunate one. This revelation somehow flattened my sense of reality, encouraged my rational approach, and confirmed my suspicion of the nonrational.

What if my mother had instead told me yet another story, one that would have led me further into the heart of the Santa Claus myth? Native peoples know this technique. They know how to point to a deeper reality when language fails. So do the great poets and the mystics. How much better it would have been if my mother had encouraged me to hold the question, to live in and with the mystery.

So, here I was again, some years later, doubting my belief in God, another story that seemed too good to be true, but this time with no one to confirm my suspicion. Likewise, my cosmic sense, so apparent to me as I remember myself lying on the front lawn, was never developed. Although liturgical reform in the Catholic Church began even before the Second Vatican Council, there were still no rituals to strengthen my natural yet fragile bonds with the cosmos. My doubts persisted like a quiet background drone for many years. The fact that I continued to pray and to live the life of a Sister of Saint Joseph shows both my attraction to the sacred and my success at repressing the dissonance.

I sense that belief is generally more difficult for scientific types like myself. I had yet to begin a career in science; however, in some ways I had my toes dangling in the trap that befalls so many scientists. We who are fascinated by matter and focused on the material side of reality for most of our day need help at times to see that there is more to life than what can be measured with a meter stick or a force sensor.

Many of the scientists that I know are agnostic, although I also interact with many who practice in one of the traditions. It seems that the great explosion of scientific knowledge over the last 150 years has created an unreal optimism about the ability of science to discover what lies at the heart of matter. So much of what was once mystery is now better understood, thanks to rapid advances by thousands of brilliant minds. Present-day explanations so far exceed their predecessors that they seem at first glance to be all encompassing. Besides, for a scientist, it is very tempting and almost natural to dream of reducing everything to the simplest set of laws. And somehow, even at this early stage, I too was enticed by the simplicity of reductionism.

I now realize that I lacked insight into both the physical and spiritual aspects of nature. I had not yet encountered chaos theory nor did I understand the emerging processes that operate within the evolving natural world. And though I had experienced the spiritual power of matter as a child, I had no idea how to name it. What I needed at this point in my journey was to experience not only the depth of the natural world but also the dynamics of the spiritual world and to be able to contemplate quietly how spirit and matter are intertwined. I needed to be encouraged to pray with nature, to return to the simplicity of that little girl on the front lawn. But all of this happened much later. Instead, I had to let my questions percolate, my doubts brew.

It was the writings of the Jesuit paleontologist Pierre Teilhard de Chardin that consoled me during these years of doubt. Despite the fact that I had difficulty grasping his imagery, which is taken largely from physics, Teilhard's great love for God, for earth, and for the cosmos, as well as his own struggle to make sense of evolution in light of the Christian tradition, oozed from his writings, warmed my heart, and satisfied my soul.

THE INNER AND OUTER JOURNEYS

As I think back over the years that intervened, I realize that one of the most important lessons of my life has been learning how my inner and outer journeys are interconnected. To be able to spiral out into a larger world, I was told, it is necessary to plunge more deeply into that inner well at the core of my being. Likewise, if I would be in touch with the core of my being, I would need to embrace, at least in desire, the entire world. There was something very alluring about both the scope and the symmetry of this suggestion, which might account for my taking it seriously.

Three aspects of my outer journey have had a profound effect on my life of faith: my journey into the field of physics brought me into the heart of the microscopic world; my journey to the Philippine Islands brought me into the heart of a culture other than my own; and my journey out through spacetime into the evolutionary universe brought me to the heart of the cosmos. During each phase of my outer journey I have been strongly motivated to deepen my understanding of God, myself, and our world. And the dissonances that I experienced along the way have provided me with clues to guide my next steps.

PHASE 1: INTO THE HEART OF MATTER

My journey into physics was motivated partly by my interest in the writings of Pierre Teilhard de Chardin. Although I thoroughly enjoyed mathematics, due mainly to my father's influence, and had always wanted to continue in its study, Teilhard's imagery alerted me to the richness of the world of physics and made me curious. Thus, my choice of physics over mathematics. As I worked through textbook assignments and poured over research problems, I came to a deeper understanding of the quantum world of matter. The beauty of the dance that elementary particles are continually executing at this level intrigued me. In contrast to my early fascination with starry skies, it was the inner world of the cosmos that was attracting me now. I loved the study of physics for its glorious explanations and elegant models, for its ability to describe all kinds of patterns in nature ranging from the vibrational modes of a drumhead to the patterns formed by electrons scattered from a crystal lattice. Yet, despite my fascination with the explanatory power of physics, I sensed that there was something missing. Perhaps it was because I had learned to appreciate the beauty and harmony created by musical patterns before I ever began writing equations to describe the physical world that I sensed a gap. This gap kept me searching for ways to connect my artistic sense, my religious sense, and my cosmic sense.

I was pursuing this study during difficult times in the Roman Catholic Church and in the religious congregation of the Sisters of Saint Joseph that I had joined after high school. The Second Vatican Council had called for deep renewal in both the local church and in religious orders. But hopes, fueled by the forward-looking documents issued by the council, were often dampened by total resistance or, at best, a very slow and reluctant response. At the same time, council documents had asked members of religious orders and congregations to examine their early histories to discern the true spirit of their founders. The results of these studies have spurred radical changes in the lifestyle of apostolic religious over the past forty years, but in those early days change was often very slow and painful, sometimes even divisive. One by one, rigid monastic structures were giving way, often with nothing substantial to replace them immediately. In the meantime there was confusion regarding the very meaning of religious life. Many departed for one reason or another, leaving those of us who stayed with even more questions.

So, in the midst of my newfound understanding of the microscopic world and burdened with the frustrations of convent life, the exhaustion of comprehensive exams, and a major flare-up of doubt, I decided to make my first directed retreat. In this type of retreat one meets each day with a director who discerns with the retreatant the movements of the spirit. On the second day of the retreat, my director suggested that for prayer I use an image that would describe my relationship with God. The next day I reluctantly shared my experience of myself as a planet on a wobbly orbit around the sun. I was afraid that, because it seemed so mechanistic and impersonal, it would disappoint my spiritual director. As it turned out, the sun continues to be a powerful image for me, one that is both relational and mutual, one that at the time opened up for me a whole new way of seeing, feeling, and relating to God, one that is ironically more personal and real.

As I contemplated the relationship of sun to earth, the sheer force of attraction between them, the tremendous outpouring of energy from the sun, the invisible shower of photons that sustain all of life on earth, my understanding of God developed and grew and eventually helped me to see God's presence in less obvious ways. This image energized me and guided me through the next several years like the star that led the Magi to the Christ Child. I was experiencing Paul's God, the Cosmic Christ, and Teilhard's God, Omega, drawing all of creation into the future by an empowering presence.

Images from science, particularly physics, continue to be very important in my faith development. Experiencing God as a force somewhat akin to gravity helps me to move beyond the masculine stereotype of God as Father. Images of light and energy, used often by the mystics of all traditions, including my own, replaced for me this single metaphor. At the same time, I realized in new ways the fact that the best we can do when we try to talk about God is to use imagery.

As a result of this retreat, I began to see how my story was connected to the great biblical epics, and my mission to the mission of Jesus. My vista expanded beyond my own neighborhood. Before beginning graduate study, I had been teaching in a poor city parish, concerned with the physical and spiritual needs of the children in my classes. Now, I was challenged to look more carefully at the structures that keep people poor, the social effects of science and technology, the global situation. I began to explore these issues and participated actively in my congregation's newly established Commission for Justice.

Looking into the heart of matter had somehow caused me to expand my vision beyond my neighborhood to the very ends of the world. This led me to the next leg of the journey. I had always had a secret desire to be a missionary to Asia. Now, it seemed right that I should put my new degree at the service of a developing country.

PHASE 2: OFF TO THE PHILIPPINES

However, as I prepared to minister in the Philippines, I was surprised to find another part of myself challenged and in need of development. Just as my probing the depths of matter had expanded my horizon for action, so now my desire to travel to the other end of the world impelled me to venture down into my inner self, to struggle with what I found there, and in the process, to work at integrating the masculine and feminine sides of my personality. Though difficult at times, this inner work was astoundingly fruitful and has convinced me of the continuing presence of God at the core of my being.

One of the byproducts of this phase was a raft of more grounded and feminine images of God, images that often emerged from my dreams. A tree that once appeared gnawed in two was transformed into a magnificent oak with roots pressing into the soil and with branches stretching toward the sun. My sky god had finally become united with my earth mother.

In *She Who Is* feminist theologian Elizabeth Johnson suggests many feminine images that reflect what she calls "a livingness in God." In her discussion of the Trinity, Johnson notes how God's presence in the universe touches us in a trinity of ways: God is "a beyond, a with, and a within to the world and its history" (210). This image presents a new way of interpreting the trinitarian mystery as well as seeing the power of God's action and presence in the world. God is beyond space and time, constantly alluring the cosmos and each one of us into a future that maximizes our potential for deep joy and personal growth. Yet God is also very close. In fact, the cosmos is nestled in God's heart. But the cosmos is also charged with God. God is at the very heart of every elementary particle, within each of us, in fact, very close to us, intimately interacting with us, in us, and through us at every moment of the day. And though this triple presence is a hidden one, it becomes vibrantly present to those who are open to seeking it.

It was also during this phase that I came to know more about my basic desire for unity. I began to notice my natural inclination to integrate things, to make connections between ideas and people, to look for the big picture, as ways of expressing this desire. This desire plays itself out in my life in a number of ways: in interests that are interdisciplinary and cross-cultural, in projects that are integrating and bonding.

When I was in high school, I wrote an essay for a high school English class on Paul's exhortation "to bring all things into one under Christ's headship" (Eph 1:10). The point of the exercise, as I remember it, had something to do with promoting missionary activity, which in those days had the rather narrow focus of converting people to the Christian way of life. For reasons that were unclear to me at the time, I found this call to unity very attractive. Although the exercise had engendered in me a deep love for this scripture passage, now, in learning to bond with persons in whose culture I suddenly found myself, I discovered its deeper dimensions. Far from being about converting people to a particular religious tradition, these words now speak to me about establishing a world order that honors the other's insights and culture. Rather than being about homogenizing, the passage is about weaving diverse strands into a complex whole. This kind of world order mirrors the kind of flexible inner order that allows a myriad of experiences and ways of approaching life to coexist and to enhance each other. I have come to call this reconciliation.

At about the same time as I was beginning to recognize my own desire, research into our early history was making it clear that the original charism of the Sisters of Saint Joseph was unity and reconciliation. This means that the mission of Jesus, the mission of my congregation, and my own inner mission are one. They complement each other in life-giving ways. This fortuitous trinity has motivated me to work at aspects of reconciliation that at times are painful and feel like too much trouble.

Again, I found myself reaching for scientific imagery to try to understand what reconciliation really means. And where else would I turn but to the stars? In the cores of these giant furnaces, hydrogen is being transformed into new elements through the process of fusion, a process that I came to recognize as a graphic image of the agony and ecstasy of reconciliation. In this process light positively charged nuclei, particles that naturally repel one another, are energized in an environment of extremely high temperature and pressure. Under these conditions, nuclei can approach close enough to one another to respond to an attractive, short-range, strong nuclear force. When they do, they form totally new entities with properties very different from those they formerly displayed. But it takes a lot of energy to overcome the long-range repulsive electric force. Only in the heat of the fire can fusion take place. In this process two become one, a differentiated other, not by sacrificing their essence but by being open to the fire and participating in an inter-particle dance.

In *The Divine Milieu* Teilhard uses another image from nature to describe the work of reconciliation:

> The labor of seaweed as it concentrates in its tissues the substances scattered, in infinitesimal quantities, throughout the vast layers of the ocean; the industry of bees as they make honey from juices broadcast in so many flowers—these are but pale images of the ceaseless work-ing-over that all the forces of the universe undergo in us in order to reach the level of spirit. (60)

Teilhard makes it clear that reconciliation is a major thrust of our earth and the evolutionary cosmos. He points out that reconciliation requires persistence. It means more than a desire. It demands the active participation of each of us in the weaving together of those especially stubborn strands of reality that continue to elude efforts at integration. In Teilhard's optimistic view, everything will eventually be bonded together in the Cosmic Christ with that illusive glue that he calls consistence.

Eventually, though, it became clear that in order to be truly authentic, my search for unity would have to start within my own person. It was only when I could actually allow the various aspects of my life, the masculine and the feminine, the scientific and the religious, my head and my heart, to coexist in a balanced way that my quest for unity began to be realized. Aspects that seemed as diverse as the squares of a patchwork quilt suddenly organized themselves into what I finally learned to see as a coherent whole. This insight then encouraged me to let the cross-cultural expressions in which I was immersed weave themselves into the patchwork of my life.

Very early during my stay in the Philippines, an incident occurred that has had a major impact on my view of the way God acts through us to bring about this type of unity. When I arrived in 1984, many groups, with a spectrum of motivations and ideologies, were already resisting the dictatorship of Ferdinand Marcos, who had been in power for about twenty years. About a year later, due to this resistance, a presidential election was called for and a few prominent church leaders began to organize the disparate resistance groups into a coherent focus. Cory Aquino, wife of opposition leader and former Senator Benigno Aquino, who had recently been assassinated, was chosen by the coalition as its presidential candidate. As expected, the election was blatantly fraudulent. As a consequence, the army revolted and millions of citizens lined the streets outside the barracks to guard the troops joining in what is now known as the People Power Revolution. After four days of growing resistance throughout the country, Marcos left the Philippines and Cory Aquino was installed as president amid great jubilation. To celebrate the victory, Freddy Aguilar, a popular songwriter at the time, composed the song "Magkaisa," which can be translated roughly as "we should become one." More than the victory of ousting a dictator, these words articulate the deep taste for unity experienced during those four glorious days in February 1986 by a people usually divided, as we all are, by ideological, geographical, and cultural differences. The euphoria that accompanied the onset of unity made the struggle worthwhile. This experience has left me with a profound understanding of the amazing self-organizing potential available to the human species if only we could learn to act as one.

PHASE 3: OUT TO THE COSMOS

On returning home from the Philippines I embarked on a third phase of my journey. I came to appreciate at a new level the breadth of the cosmos in both time and space with special thanks again to Teilhard, to my growing understanding of astronomy and modern cosmology, and this time to Passionist Father Thomas Berry and the many others who have been reflecting on Teilhard's work and developing it. Though I obviously had encountered the Big Bang and other details of the great story of the universe in my study of physics, it was only now that I began to contemplate the story, to internalize something of its almost fourteen billion year history and its creative, evolutionary processes. As I reflected on the story, I could imagine the tremendous power that, at the beginning of time, burst forth in every direction and the energy that was released as protons fused into helium. I was able to feel the slowness of galaxy formation. I watched the cosmos expand and cool and recycle matter in second- and third-generation stars. I realized that it is in this context that the unity that I seek is best achieved. The story of the universe verified my intuition that we are one after all.

To be able to describe the various stages of cosmic evolution and to know that mathematical and scientific models exist to confirm the plausibility of all of this is thrilling. The capacity to see God's spirit present within each moment of cosmic activity is profound. If we know how to interpret their findings, it is the scientists who are revealing aspects of the beauty, grandeur, and power of the divine that we could never have imagined in earlier times.

Insights into the dynamic processes that continue to move the cosmos forward have provided me with a startlingly new context to view my life, the universe, and God. They have helped me to understand better why sorrow, pain, and death must be part of an unfinished world. They have led me to experience God both dwelling at the heart of the cosmos and alluring the cosmos into the future. They have consolidated my faith and given me a greater sense of God's action in the world. They have encouraged me to search through my own life to find similar patterns in my life story.

A recent rereading of many of Teilhard's religious essays has led me to notice an image that brings greater clarity to the cosmic unity that we experience (see Fabel and St. John 2003). I call this image the cosmic tapestry. Throughout his many religious essays, Teilhard refers often to fibers and threads. He explains in his major work, *The Human Phenomenon,* that these threads are not fibers of silk or nylon but the curves formed when the positions of the elementary particles of the early universe are plotted against time. As particles are attracted and repelled in spacetime, their spacetime plot weaves a tapestry of increasing complexity. Cross-sections of this plot portray a record of the evolutionary process at single instants in time. As time goes by, these threads weave themselves into what appear in the cross-sections to be atoms, molecules, cells, tissue, plants, and animals, always more complex organisms.

Teilhard visualizes threads of spirit interacting and weaving in complementary ways. In fact, for him, matter and spirit provide the warp and weft of this evolving tapestry. Threads of matter form a matrix which supports and is supported by these similarly emerging threads of spirit. Teilhard uses this visual image to support his hunch that the universe is being gradually drawn into greater and greater complexity by Omega, the Cosmic Christ, who holds the tapestry together.

The image of a cosmic tapestry has further unified my view of the cosmos and has provided me with the basis for a cosmic spirituality. It helps me to focus my attention on the interconnection of everything within the cosmos, the spiritual power of matter, the importance of relationship. It describes my own experiences of growth and diminishment. And it has been my privilege in recent years to be able to share the power of this image as well as the story of the universe with others.

As I continue to contemplate and to tell this great story to others, I am becoming more aware of the fundamental dynamic inherent in the cosmos that governs its evolution. Thomas Berry has extracted from Teilhard's writings three fundamental principles that govern the universal becoming: differentiation, subjectivity, and communion. These principles are somewhat akin to spiritual movements in that they guide the creative activity of the universe and propel it onward. They operate on all levels, within every creature. They have been operating from the beginning of time and are responsible for the novelty that we experience in the ongoing story of evolution. For anyone who wishes to go deeper in these matters, I suggest Brian Swimme's and Thomas Berry's *The Universe Story* (1992).

A reading of the fusion process that I described above in the light of these principles might go something like this. Protons, like humans, have a spiritual nature, albeit one that is not so highly developed as it is in humans. However, these morsels of spirit are enough for them to allow the natural, repulsive tendency that they feel in the presence of other positively charged particles to be overcome. In some limited way protons relate to one another as subject and, when the physical conditions are right, unite with one another in communion. In the process they differentiate and become something new—deuterium—adding to the diversification and complexification of the cosmos. Their newness results from the union of two distinct entities that, while retaining their identity, reach beyond themselves to become one.

The governing principles of differentiation, subjectivity, and communion reveal universal tendencies in nature. Their pattern can be found in many other earth processes: the formation of the water molecule from hydrogen and oxygen atoms, the union of sperm and egg, the experience of human love. They act on all levels: physical, chemical, biological, social, and spiritual. I find that understanding how these principles operate on the physical level keeps me connected to the cosmos, helps me to understand the cosmic movements in my life, and provides a valuable key to discernment.

I know, for instance, the long, slow process of formation that mirrors that of the stars. Like the proton in the process of fusion, I know the struggle inherent in working toward reconciliation. Like the enriched gas and dust from first- and second-generation stars that occupy vast regions of space forming into protostars, I know the cycle of birth and death that continues to recycle matter and conceive more complex entities. I also know the creative spark that can trigger a new way of being. I find that looking for these movements in my own life and learning how to proceed in such situations from the lessons of cosmic history help me to cooperate with that innate potential within each of us that continually moves us as members of the cosmos toward greater unity.

The great story of the universe also demands that I question what it means to act ethically in a universe where everything is filled with a sacred presence and has been uniquely formed during an unrepeatable evolutionary process. It draws my attention to the damage that the human community is doing to planet earth when we consume more than our share of fossil fuels, pollute the environment, waste precious resources, and destroy endangered species. It points out the necessity of adopting a sustainable-future approach rather than a profit-oriented one. It shows that humanity, as earth conscious of herself, must act.

Without such a story it would be difficult to be motivated enough to implement the kind of social and political change needed for the reconciliation not only of neighbor with neighbor, of nation with nation, but also of the human species with the rest of creation. The story of the universe, on the other hand, provides a marvelous stimulus for a change of lifestyle and offers valuable lessons for living gently on earth.

BRINGING IT ALL TOGETHER

Today, as I continue my journey, I continue to describe my personal mission in terms of reconciliation: the personal reconciliation of heart with head, the reconciliation of science with religion, the reconciliation of matter with spirit.

My personal experience has been that faith is developmental and can grow only if it is nurtured and challenged by the events of everyday life, its joys and suffering, the knowledge that I acquire, the relationships that I form. For me, faith is facilitated when I see the many aspects of my life woven into a single fabric. It is deepened when the focus of my life becomes the Divine Attractor. A relationship with God, like any relationship, requires patience and practice, commitment and trust. It means coming to know myself, imperfect but loved, falling short but full of desire. It is only in seeing how the work that God does in my inner being is reflected in the evolutionary processes of the cosmos that I am able to grasp and be grasped by the God of evolution.

Technology has provided us with wonderful ways of coming to know the cosmos more deeply. But the irony is that it has also separated us from nature in many ways. I find that my relationship with the cosmos, with earth, with nature is only developed when I spend time with nature, enjoying the night sky, identifying birds, gardening, smelling the flowers. It is only when I spend time outdoors, in nature, that I have been able to experience the remarkable joy and freedom that accompany a cosmic sense.

My own experience, of doubt and of early questioning of the existence of God, motivates me to continue to exert what effort I can in the burgeoning science-and-religion dialogue. I see this as a way to encourage others and to participate myself in the renewal of the religious traditions that have provided us with such wisdom throughout the ages.

My Roman Catholic tradition has a long history with roots that extend back beyond the patriarch, Abraham. The wisdom stored in this tradition about the meaning of life is rich. I am strengthened and inspired by it. However, the fact that the official Catholic Church continues to deny women access to the priesthood and other forms of power saddens me. It also saddens me that so few of our theologians have taken up the challenge presented by modern science and tried to make sense of recent discoveries. Many of our parishioners are still interpreting Genesis in a way that keeps it unnecessarily in conflict with evolution. There is very little nuanced exploration of the ethical issues connected to breakthroughs in biotechnology. I also regret that so little is being done in the local church to encourage a cosmic sense through ritual, symbol, and story. Instead, these have lost much of their power. The ancient religions began in the forest, with people looking at the sky. It seems natural that spiritual development should begin with our being in touch with the beauties and processes of nature. As Ignatius of Loyola demonstrates in the final contemplation of *The Spiritual Exercises*, this kind of spirituality leads to an ability to see God in all things, which is radically different from either pantheism or earth worship (for the text of the *Exercises*, see Ganss 1991).

Contemplating the story of the universe and telling it to others is one practical way for me to share the power that scientific metaphors have for our living, the great parallels that exist between each individual story and this great story. Recently, a friend and I have been doing just that in a variety of formats: retreats, classes, talks. We encourage participants to notice the connections that can be made between each person's personal story and this great epic so that each of us can begin to access the depths of the potential that is ours and to develop a relationship with earth that is mutual.

In the classes, retreats, and other presentations that I offer on the story of the universe and the work of Teilhard de Chardin, I encourage participants to consider the sacred nature of our place in the cosmos and hope that they will look even a bit more reverently on our earth as subject. I have found, to my surprise, that I have not been alone all these years. Many who attend these programs have shared personal stories similar to mine. I learned that the number of us who have a secret love for nature, for earth, and for the universe is legion.

Of course, through all of these years, I realize that one of my greatest resources has been my life as a member of the Sisters of Saint Joseph, a true community of faith. I am grateful for the opportunities that living in a faith community provide. Daily community prayer, frequent faith sharing and eucharistic liturgy, spiritual direction and yearly retreats nurture my desire to know the Divine. And I am grateful for the amazing changes that we as a congregation have made, not without great struggle, to bring our mission and lifestyle to its present state.

I am particularly grateful to my congregation for its recent articulation of our vision in which we commit ourselves not only to a contemplative lifestyle but also to those who are poor, the prophetic voice of women, and the love and care for earth. Coupled with our charism of unity and reconciliation, this corporate vision provides me with the group support that I need to carry on my own personal mission.

CONCLUSION

Questions about the origin of the universe led me to question the existence of God. A closer look at the dynamics of the universe has convinced me of the presence of God within them from the beginning of time but particularly drawing all of creation to a future full of promise. Faith is a risk. However, faith in the alluring presence of God provides me with a richer view of life, I would argue, than one empty of God. In this regard, I agree with John Haught, who asserts that both materialist and literalist interpretations of life and evolution flatten our view of the cosmos and deprive it of its characteristic depth (Haught 2003).

Truly integrated persons are those who can hold many questions in their heart. Questions about the way Santa travels on Christmas night, questions about the origin of the universe, questions about God, questions about social change, questions about the meaning of life, questions about death. They are able to access both heart and head as they contemplate these great mysteries of life. Seen in the proper light, their questions can draw them as fully human persons into the beauty of the cosmos, can pierce for them the heart of the great mystery. In this spirit I continue to pray for that kind of unity, for what Etty Hillesum calls a "thinking heart" (Gaarlandt 1985, 209).

2

The Legacy of the Mimosa Tree

LOUISE M. TEMPLE

To acknowledge that which we cannot see,
to give definition to that which we do not know,
to create divine order out of chaos,
is the religious dance.
　　　　　—Terry Tempest Williams, Refuge

INTRODUCTION

It was in the mimosa tree one hot July evening that into my consciousness popped the realization that Mama and Daddy were Santa Claus. I remember crying a little, then going to them on the little back porch of our house and announcing that I had figured it out. The mimosa tree was a favorite solitary location for me during my childhood years. It had very smooth, cool bark, and the limbs were wide enough, low and branched, that I could sit comfortably in many spots. It was in this same tree that I also spent many hours thinking about life and memorizing verses from the Bible, part of my early religious training. Born into a Christian family with deep historical and personal roots in its faith, I was nurtured through my youth by my extended family and inspired church leaders in a way that provided me a spiritual foundation that has stayed with me for life. Both my professional life occupations, scientist and musician, emerged from my religious training and experiences.

RELIGIOUS EDUCATION

The ancient biblical proverb—

> Train children in the right way,
> and when old, they will not stray (Prv 22:6)

—is full of meaning for me. I grew up in the First Baptist Church of Ruston, Louisiana. It was unusual in the Southern Baptist Convention. Ruston is a college town, home of Louisiana Tech University, and First Baptist was a popular place for college students, many faculty member families, and lots of others from the community. The story goes that in the early 1900s the church was expelled from our local Baptist association due to receiving into its membership a fellow Baptist from the Dunkard Church who had been baptized facing forward rather than backward. We were also in trouble with many community folk in the 1950s when the amazing choir from Grambling College, a neighboring black school, came to sing at a service. I remember the singing they did—which is unrivaled in my mind by anything I've heard since. And I believe they came to sing for us annually for a few years. I didn't know at the time that this practice was frowned upon, or even that is was unusual. The Rev. Dr. Avery Lee, the pastor of our church, was apparently "color blind," and he truly appreciated good music of many types, as evidenced by the musicians who served in that church and in the church he later pastored (and which I attended) in New Orleans.

This unusual Baptist congregation was the kind that would call Dr. Lee to be its pastor. He was also unusual; for example, he had received his seminary training at Yale Divinity School. I remember nothing of what he said, specifically, in his sermons, although I must have heard him preach at least 1,250 sermons—church services happened frequently in the Baptist church during those years. I do remember one rather dramatic sermon he preached at the St. Charles Ave. Baptist Church, New Orleans, called "The Impossible Dream," during which the contralto soloist performed the song by the same name from the musical "Man of LaMancha." I remember his benediction, "May the Lord bless you and keep you. May the Lord lift his countenance upon you and give you peace." It seemed normal to me at the time; only later did I learn that this particular formal benediction was probably not pronounced in any other Southern Baptist church. I remember the wonderful speakers he invited for our revivals, and the hot chocolate and donuts that we always had before the early morning revival services that I attended with my father. And I remember the dignity and reverence of the services. Dr. Lee baptized me by immersion at the age of eight, an event I remember clearly and fondly.

Dr. Lee's theology, which I know about only by reading his books, since I don't recall anything specific that he said during the years he was my pastor, is a gospel of tolerance, service, optimism, love for all people, and openness to fresh insights and inspiration from God. The books include one written in 1967, *What's Right with the Church,* and another from 1991, *Affirmations of a Skeptical Believer.* My parents' theology and life practice is similar. They must have found kindred spirits in Avery and Ann Lee. Ann was a living saint, charismatic and tireless in her enthusiasm for nurturing our faith journeys. She was the leader of the Girls' Auxiliary, my church's young women's organization, in which she inspired us young ladies to learn about missions, do outreach projects, have "Bible drills," and study the structure of our denomination. Periodically, having attained certain goals, such as memorizing the scriptures, we demonstrated our skills before a large audience of church members, amid much formality and celebration, for which I'm sure she made all the arrangements. In my memory, she was our only leader, and we often spent time at her house doing many of the activities, which she must have been supervising while caring for her three young children. When I was in my early twenties, I again worked with Ann in New Orleans, this time as a young adult leader of a Girls' Auxiliary group. She always had an optimistic and bright outlook, even through the final stages of terminal cancer later in life. Because my path crossed that of Avery and Ann Lee again during my graduate school years in New Orleans, this couple, besides my parents and grandparents, were my major spiritual mentors for all the significant years of youth and young adulthood.

Although I can't remember the explicit teachings from my pastors or teachers in my early Christian education, I do know that I learned a lot of scriptures and sang many hymns over and over again—the words describing many aspects of our faith and lives as Christians. I know that I was encouraged to base my life decisions and attitudes on the teachings of Jesus Christ and the examples he put forward during his short earthly life. I know for sure that I was taught to "work out [my] own salvation" (Phil 2:12) and that the believer and the Bible were sufficient to learn the essentials of the Christian life. I was also encouraged by word and example to use the great Bible scholars as sources for understanding the meaning of the scriptures. I was never taught that the Bible is "inerrant," meaning that it must be interpreted literally in order to be valid. Thus I was spared such problems as the necessity to believe that a human could be swallowed up by a sea-going creature and arrive some time later alive and well on a distant shore. I could instead focus on what such a story must have meant to its writers and what I might glean from it for myself.

I was taught that the Bible must be good for all time and all peoples. Written by humans for humans, it must express timeless truths that can work for all different societies. I believe God is constantly being revealed through people—the Bible is not the sole source of revelation. For these reasons I can read such startling books as those by Bishop John S. Spong (for example, *Why Christianity Must Change or Die* and *Rescuing the Bible from Fundamentalism*) without being upset, even though they advocate interpreting the scriptures in a historical manner more strict than is the norm in the churches. I think this kind of examination is acceptable, because if the Christian faith and teachings can't stand up to such scrutiny and last for all time, then this religion is inadequate and should be abandoned.

In the course of thinking about and writing this chapter, I have reconnected with my spiritual mentor from those early years. In January 2003 I was in New Orleans for a professional meeting and took a couple of hours to ride the streetcar out to St. Charles Avenue Baptist Church to visit with Avery Lee—now retired but still a greeter for the Sunday morning service. That contact started a correspondence between us that has helped me reflect

on my spiritual roots. Thanks to that encounter I read some of Avery's recent books, in which he describes his life in the context of historical events of
nine decades of the last century and explains what his basic beliefs are (see
Lee 1993). I was astounded to see my own beliefs articulated beautifully,
very much as I would have written them. This apparent "inheritance" of
beliefs reminded me of my favorite example of how strong biological inheritance is: my uncle and my father, now eighty-six and ninety years old, have
continued to grow more and more like my grandfather in their way of speaking and their mannerisms, although he has been dead for over thirty years!
Since it appears that I have adopted the same belief system as my spiritual
mentor and family, as described below, does this mean I have just absorbed
it all unquestioningly? Hardly, as I have experienced thirty-five years of my
own adult life independent of this particular leadership, and I have indeed
worked out my own belief system. But it does mirror that described by Avery
Lee in a remarkable way.

So, I believe one's early religious education plays a major role in lifelong
beliefs. Thus it has been in part my Christian training, in the context I have
described, among people who believed fervently and practiced Christian teachings in their everyday lives, that has held me constant in the faith all my life.
Other "giants" of the faith were in my own family.

FAMILY

I am named for both of my grandmothers, Mattie Lou Daniel and Marga-
ret Louise Temple—saints in their own time. I learned a reverence for life
and age from them. Their memory bespeaks a line from an unpublished
poem by Van Temple entitled "Windows to the Soul": "A Grandmother's
faith inherited by a child. The wisdom of ages unexpectantly passed on."
When my father's mother was eighty something, my grandfather died. Because she was so devoted to him, she wished to die, also. I visited her a few
months after his death and found her waiting for death. After a few more
months, I think she figured out that she wasn't going to die after all and that
she should figure out how to live. That she did very successfully until she
was a few months shy of her one-hundredth birthday. Inspiring? Yes. She
taught me to cherish life and to be devoted to my family.

My maternal grandmother's talent for teaching lured me to her Sunday
School class of adult ladies even when I was a child, visiting with her as I
often did. Her words were magic. Every Christmas, with the family gathered
around, she would recite the Christmas story from the Gospel of Luke. She
also recited poetry. Intelligent and courageous, she left her home in rural
northern Louisiana to join two of her brothers at Western Kentucky Teachers College, where she received a certificate at age eighteen. She returned to
teach for a number of years in Arcadia, my mother's hometown, until seven
years after her marriage to my grandfather when my aunt was born. From
then on she taught in less formal ways until the day she died: cooking, sewing,

manners, traditions—and spirituality—a reverence for people and God and the world. I used to sleep in the bed with Mama Lou, the name all her grandchildren called her, after Daddy Leo died. She was always incredulous that I would want to sleep with her, since she was a champion snorer. I perfected the art of stopping her snoring so I could sleep, but I had to sleep with her. I wanted to be physically close to her.

Mama Lou's life was a constant inspiration to me, and we were close friends. She imparted to me much wisdom, although I can't tell you many specifics. I picked it up "by osmosis," as the saying goes—although there is little scientific backing to that figure of speech. More aptly, she poured herself into the soul of my being through the pores in my skin. We are connected in a strong spiritual bond. She was dying in 1981 when I was traveling from Washington with my three children to begin my new life as a single mom. My mother let her know that we were coming, and she hung on to life until a few hours after our short visit one night in June. She stayed alive to make that last personal, physical contact with her spiritually connected granddaughter.

Spirituality is being open to things, ideas, people—looking for good things everywhere around you. I could never "meditate" in the classical sense of the word—I fall asleep too easily and have never done the work necessary to overcome this tendency. But I consider myself to be meditating or praying constantly, always in touch with my spiritual mentors: my grandmothers, my religious mentors, my parents, and even now awaiting new sources. It seems as though I find out a lot about myself not from introspection and self-examination but from other people. For example, when I was thirty-four years old, I was introducing my Lutheran pastor as our new chaplain for the new American Guild of Organists chapter I had guided into existence. Pastor Fjelstad thanked me for the introduction, then responded with some kind words about me, including the statement, "Louise makes things happen." Of course he was correct—I had been "making things happen" all my life, but I never thought of myself as having that characteristic. Similarly, one day a few years later, I discovered from an Episcopal priest for whom I was a frequent substitute organist that I am "always expecting something new" in all life experiences and in all people. I am constantly looking for and expecting to get insights, ideas, and inspiration from other people and the natural world. For me, this is spirituality—believing that the creation holds its revelation for all of us.

So my grandmothers both passed on their wisdom, inspiration, and spirituality to me. My grandfathers also were both strong, spiritual Christians, living their faith by example. My own parents? They provided a wealth of Christian training, mostly teaching by example. Mom and Dad were leaders in the church and faithfully took us children to worship, youth activities, and special events. Dad was a choir member until his hearing got too bad in his late seventies. The Bible was read to us at home, and personal study was encouraged. Our lives centered around church activities, and most of our friends were Christians. My parents taught me by example to respect all people as equals. For some of my childhood years we had an African American woman who ironed for us. I often went with Mama to deliver the ironing in the "colored" section of our town, and I got to know Marianna Mayfield and her family very well. I saw my mother treat this hired help with the same respect she showed her friends and family. After Marianna moved to California, my mother corresponded with her and her family for a number of years. In many other ways my parents showed me that a life based on Christian principles is a happy, fulfilling life, regardless of the external circumstances.

So, did I simply inherit my faith? No, that is not possible, but I did certainly have a fertile field provided for me in my childhood for learning about Christianity as a way of life. Although I lived until I was twenty-one years old in a very protected, provincial environment, I was somehow prepared for discovering the wider world and many differences from my familiar environment. I gradually came to know that many people were raised very differently from me and saw life in very different ways. For example, homosexuality was never discussed in my family, at church, or even at school. So you might expect that discovery of this phenomenon and learning that people you know see themselves as homosexual might have been a shocking and distressing event. I recall no such disillusioning revelations in my youth or adulthood, making me angry and bitter, as happens to many people. Why was I not traumatized by these discoveries, as many people are? I wonder if it was not the deep-seated tolerance and openness to new ideas that had been taught me by word and example. I sometimes think I lived a very protected early life—almost like being in a cocoon. But somehow I was prepared for life rather than being protected from it. I was taught the equality of all people and the love of God for everyone. Those tenets allow for many different expressions of humanity. Because there was no conflict between my religious beliefs and what I saw in the world, I did not have to choose one or the other. Instead, my religious beliefs and life philosophy support my pleasure in and curiosity about the natural world.

Many people are nurtured in their faith during childhood but fall away from it sometime later in life. They have a crisis of their belief system when they are removed from the "womb" of family and home religious institutions. Some leave the church and their faith, never to return. Others find their way back to Christianity through a route of their own making, perhaps influenced by people outside their families. Even within my own family, some have decided they no longer believe in God or the teachings of Jesus. So, the decision, which in truth is simply a decision, to continue believing is not totally dependent on one's early Christian education and family environment.

I no longer worship as a Southern Baptist, having belonged to several other Christian denominations in the last thirty-five years, including the Lutheran and the Episcopal. Some of the reasons for abandoning the Baptists were practical, some theological, and some personal taste in the worship experience. The only factor of relevance here is that I found as an adult that the Baptist training emphasized the singular "rightness" of Baptist beliefs, even though the individual believer was really quite independent and personally responsible. I resented that I was never taught to appreciate the role of the Roman Catholic and Eastern churches in maintaining the Christian religion for over a thousand years. After studying Christian history in college, experiencing different worship styles, and learning about other Christian traditions, I came to appreciate how much we all have in common in our beliefs. I have a strong ecumenical philosophy that says that there should be many groups and styles of worship among Christians, all of whom should respect the choices of others who have the same basic faith. Only in this way can we as Christians possibly accomplish the good things that are needed in our communities and the world.

As I grew older and entered my independent adult life, I maintained my Christian faith as the foundation of my life and the basis of my life philosophy. I had a number of other outstanding spiritual mentors in several Christian denominations and enjoyed rich and rewarding friendships with fellow Christians through the years. I have a gift of receptiveness and openness to learning from individuals and situations, so I have found many expressions of and gifts from God through my church and other life experiences. A major expression of my own faith experience has come through music.

MUSIC

There is an old saying that "God gave us music that we might pray without words." It has meant a lot to me. Music and church went hand in hand. I sang a lot from an early age; I can still sing many of the wonderful hymns from my youth, all four verses, by memory! I began taking piano lessons at age eight. When I could play the hymns on the piano, I was asked to play along with the organist for the Sunday evening service. I sang in or accompanied choirs in both school and church throughout my school years, then in church choirs throughout my adult life. I was unwittingly pulled into organ playing by a high school friend, Nancy Byrd, a wonderful contralto whom I often accompanied in her singing. She would agree to sing at a friend's wedding, then announce that she had the organist, and I would end up playing for the wedding. However, I did not study organ formally until I was twenty-eight and pregnant with my second daughter. I truly cannot remember what inspired me to start lessons; it was almost like I had gotten a message telling me to do it. Furthermore, I seemed to know where to look for a very good teacher; I found him at an Episcopal church in Newport, Rhode Island, where I was living at the time. He took me on as a student, and before my baby was born, he had taught me Anglican chant and I was playing alternate Sundays at a small Episcopal church in a nearby community. That was the beginning of over forty years of studying organ, learning choral directing, and participating as an organist and choir director in many churches and a few synagogues.

Music has kept me involved in the church more consistently than any other aspect of religion. I chuckled when I recently read a similar thought in one of G. Avery Lee's books, one written long after he had retired from active ministry: "To tell the truth, the music is a main reason that I go to church" (Lee 1993). Because of my lifelong participation in the music portion of worship, I can see so many ways that the faith is taught and expressed and shared through this venue. For me, music is my deepest religious expression. Nothing brings me more joy than playing a beautiful hymn with a meaningful text that often comes directly from scripture, in a way that encourages worshipers to sing and praise God for their own spiritual enrichment. All emotions and feelings can be captured in some kind of musical expression—from the depths of sadness to the heights of ecstasy. Music provides means of expression that simply cannot be found in any other medium.

How could such beauty have been inspired? Christian composers through the ages have expressed their deep religious convictions and experiences. Johann Sebastian Bach, whose organ and choral music are my favorites, was a deeply religious person. I think with awe and wonder of the depth and extent of inspiration for such giant composers of Christian music, who derived this inspiration from their own beliefs and spirituality. I also wonder why this particular human activity or skill ever developed at all. A similar sentiment was noted in a newspaper article that observed:

> The ability to enjoy music has long puzzled biologists because it does nothing evident to help survival. Why, therefore, should evolution have built into the human brain this soul-stirring source of pleasure? Man's faculties for enjoying and producing music, Darwin wrote, "must be ranked among the most mysterious with which he is endowed." (Wade 2003)

I am now a music minister—a title I obtained with absolutely no formal training in ministry simply by accepting a position in a small Lutheran parish in suburban New Jersey. My mission there is to provide the best hymns and liturgical music for the faith expression of the worshipers and to find ways for everyone to share his or her musical gifts in worship. As professional church workers know, being a church employee, and particularly being the musician, often obstructs one's own religious and worship experiences. There is a great potential for becoming cynical and disillusioned and losing one's own faith. However, I find that I am more enriched by the experience than I am drained by it. For a number of years I served as a regular substitute or interim organist in a variety of churches. I found this to be a very enriching experience, probably because I was open to and looking for spiritual gifts from others. Those years helped me to see the common beliefs and practices that are so strong across all denominations. In my present position I am often tired by Thursday nights and really don't want to conduct a choir rehearsal. Of course I go and have the rehearsal, and almost every time I leave refreshed and inspired by the dedication and devotion of my choristers. I do minister to them in many ways, and they in turn minister to me. On balance, my faith has been strengthened by my work in church music.

Over twenty years ago I found myself in need of a career to support myself and my children, and I pondered whether to pursue music or science. I had considerable training in both but questioned whether I really was prepared for a good job in either. I opted to pursue graduate studies in science, specifically microbiology and biochemistry, thinking that it would be easier to make a living as a scientist than as a church musician. That decision allowed me to continue doing church music but took me professionally toward my teaching career in biology.

SCIENCE

Ursula Goodenough once wrote that "the role of religion is to integrate the Cosmology and the Morality, to render the cosmological narrative so rich and compelling that it elicits our allegiance and our commitment to its emergent moral understandings" (Goodenough 1998). I came to be a scientist by a route that directly involved my religious experiences. Medical missionaries who visited our church often and shared their experiences inspired me to announce when I was twelve that I wanted to be a medical missionary. I guess this phenomenon is common, as I've heard of many young Catholic girls who aspired to be nuns. At that early age I had figured out that the best way to do missions was to try and meet the critical needs of the people with whom one was hoping to share the Christian gospel, so it was medical missions or no missions for me. This must not have been a truly inspired calling, as the vision dimmed during college—but I mention this since it is the way I got into science. I did get to experience a taste of the medical missions experience in Africa during a 1969 summer stint in what was then Rhodesia. My husband at the time was a fourth-year medical student and I, a medical technologist. We both worked that summer in a rural mission hospital where I served as the lab technician, assisted by a severely humpbacked local woman. In spite of the positive nature of this experience, I became convinced that I did not want to do foreign missions as a career. While I was an adventurous person, I had some philosophical differences with the imposition of the Western cultural aspects of Christianity onto the native cultures. For example, in the region where I worked, village chiefs who became Christian had to choose only one of their several wives, and the others no longer had a place in the community. Not all missionaries that I met agreed with these decisions, but it was a policy of the Mission Board. Barbara Kingsolver's recent best seller, *Poisonwood Bible*, illustrates some of what I experienced.

I attended Mississippi College, a Baptist liberal-arts school near Jackson, Mississippi. I chose this school not because it was religious based but for two other distinct reasons. First, since I aspired to go to medical school, I chose it because of its pre-medical program and success rate in medical school acceptance. Second, and perhaps more important, my grandfather had taught mathematics at Mississippi College some thirty or more years earlier, years that served as a stepping stone on his journey from the farm in northern Mississippi to graduate school in Texas and a career in college teaching. This family connection drew me strongly to Mississippi College. It was a great choice for me. I participated in the life of the campus, not bothered by the rather restrictive set of rules, including obligatory chapel attendance. I sang in one of the choirs, attended the local Baptist church, and studied hard to finish my pre-medical requirements in three years. Here, as in my earlier training, I remember no attempts to teach us a single way to believe.

My zoology teacher, "Doc" Sadler, a legend in Mississippi College history, may have been an atheist. At least he did not attend the local church where many faculty members worshiped. As far as I remember, however, he never brought religion into the classroom. Doc was an inspired, demanding teacher. He hammered home the concept that "ontogeny recapitulates phylogeny"—meaning that the embryogenesis is a telescoped version of evolution. This phrase should not be interpreted too broadly, but there are many elements of embryogenesis that do mirror the evolutionary process as we understand it. It was in Doc Sadler's classes that I was first taught about evolution, and it made perfect sense to me. The so-called conflict between religion and science, mostly in reference to evolution, had not erupted full-blown at that time. My training in science at Mississippi College was excellent and prepared me well for graduate education.

I left graduate school after two years in medicine and a biochemistry graduate program to marry and support my husband in his medical education. I was doing well in school but found the pressures of being a woman in the male-dominated arena of medical education too stressful for me. After our first child was born, I worked only part time, occasionally, in hospital laboratories. Over twelve years later, after the DNA revolution had changed the study of nearly everything within cells, I returned to graduate school and obtained a master's degree and a doctorate in chemistry and microbiology, respectively. After a few years of postdoctoral work and teaching, I took a position at Drew University in the Department of Biology.

How does my scientific training and career as an educator mesh with my religious training? Teaching, for me, is a direct extension of my life philosophy, which is based on Christian teachings. I look at all students as individuals, try to understand something about who they are, how they function best, and how much challenge versus support they need. I try to discern how they learn and function best. I share my excitement about cellular function and all its ramifications, and I watch as they catch that spirit and experience it for themselves. I take this responsibility—the care and nurturing of my students—very seriously, but my enjoyment and pleasure in the process are immense.

As a scientist, I study things that I can't see—like DNA and proteins. All subcellular structures are invisible to the eye, and many are invisible by microscopy as well. We have some pretty good ideas of what biological macromolecules (DNA, protein, lipids, conglomerates of these) look like—by virtue of seeing a pattern of electron-spray from coating the objects with dense material that deflects electrons. But visualizing the actual molecules is beyond our current capabilities. Similarly, many things in science are accepted as realities when we haven't really "proven" them beyond any doubt. On the other side of the coin, many scientists feel strongly that they cannot believe in something that cannot be tested or proven to be true, and that the burden of proof of "spiritual" claims lies with the believer. In the words of the scientist-philosopher Alan Cromer: "Until the evidence is there, the only sane course is to reject all claims that are unverified and inconsistent with current knowledge" (Cromer 1993). The problem with such an approach, in my opinion, is that scientists deny the validity of observations simply because they cannot find any means of explaining them. Experimental studies of "spiritual" effects on healing, for example, are difficult to design. Nevertheless, a number of studies on the effect of prayer in healing showed a positive correlation of statistical significance and "given that approximately 57% of trials showed a positive treatment effect, the evidence thus far merits further study" (see Matthews et al. 2000).

Scientists of every age have been curious and full of questions; at the same time they are often confident to the point of being arrogant about their understanding of some aspect of nature. So far, no generation of scientists has been correct about everything. Many reverently held "dogmas" have been debunked with more sophisticated equipment and techniques. Just because we know more than our predecessors does not mean that we are correct about everything we now believe to be true. Each group of scientists is hampered in its quest for answers by limited technology and equipment, by failure to ask the questions that might reveal interesting and important observations, and by previous prejudicial information that blinds it to evidence that might otherwise be obvious.

There are many areas of scientific inquiry in which we are just scratching the surface of understanding. One of these is the brain and nervous system. While we have made incredible strides, it is still a great frontier of science. As a cell biologist expressed it, "Neuroscientists in fact have as yet little to tell us about love or joy or astonishment, and they are unlikely to have much to say until they understand how consciousness (self-awareness) is produced in brains" (in Goodenough 1998). When we have probed to the point where we feel certain of most fundamentals of the workings of the human mind, will we then start developing tools to study these emotional and spiritual aspects? How about trying to understand such non-Western medical procedures as acupuncture? Those events and observations that simply are not explicable by any means we've uncovered so far? I think we may never fully understand the mysteries of the creation we live in; there will always be more questions to ask and try to answer. Is this the spirit of "God" in us?

Often people think that scientists cannot be religious because of a perceived conflict between religion and the scientific view of evolution. I have students ask me how I am able to reconcile what appear to be two different belief systems. Science is a belief system in that we "believe" we understand how something occurs in the natural world, but when further understanding develops, we modify or change our "belief." How can I not be religious, for all the reasons I have already described, and how can I fail to believe in evolution when I see evidence of it all around me? I can watch evolution happen in my bacteria practically before my eyes. For me, however, there is no conflict. When you are never taught that the Bible is a scientific document—when, in fact, you are taught that much of the Bible is allegory and parables—you never seem to run into problems of conflict with observations about the natural world. Do we as scientists understand all the details and fine points of the evolutionary process? Certainly not. There are gaps in our knowledge of evolution, between humanoids and other mammals, as well as in other areas of the animal, plant, and microbial kingdoms. Even if we could prove with fossil evidence a smooth evolutionary line, other kinds of questions remain that cannot be answered with fossil evidence. Are humans with their highly developed intellectual systems a quirk in the evolutionary process? Are we here on earth as the result of some nonhuman intervention? A lot of my current thinking has to do with the role of humans in the evolutionary process, because we are having a major effect on the world in which we live. I wonder what the ultimate end of the evolution of life on earth may be. Will we control ourselves enough to make the planet sustainable? Are we "evolving" the earth in a new kind of evolution, but a kind that was inevitable from the start, given our mental capabilities? Did God will the human race into being to destroy the earth? These are the questions that we scientists with religious beliefs should be and are grappling with.

I don't do my thinking in mimosa trees as an adult, but I do revisit the mimosa tree every year in one of my science classes. It turns out that the leaf of this tree has an unusual characteristic: the leaflets all close together when touched. I use this example as a context for describing a very intricate and complex cell signaling mechanism that is well understood in many, but not all, aspects. Our scientific knowledge is like this example; we understand so much, but gaps remain. Those gaps may be much larger than we currently imagine, but we, as curious and inquisitive human beings, will continue to search out answers to our scientific questions. When we gain understanding, then will the "magic" be gone? No more than is the joy of giving and receiving gone when the myth of Santa fades during childhood. I have chosen over and over again throughout my life to maintain a belief system that in all the fundamental ways matches what I was taught as a child. This belief system is congruent with my scientific training, because, as a scientist in the twenty-first century, I know we do not fully understand the natural world and the place of humans in it.

TO BELIEVE OR NOT BELIEVE

Why do I still believe? "Why not?" I said, only half jokingly, when first confronted with this question. My faith is something I was practically born with. I had an incredibly solid Christian education and was inspired during my youth by giants of the faith, both in my family and outside. Believing in a Creator, a Supreme Being, a spiritual dimension to life: all of these require a conscious decision on the part of a modern educated person. For me, such belief fits together well in all aspects of my life and training. Humans "in the image of God" express truths of God's nature. My understanding of God gives me a great sense of awe in the creation. Music is an incredibly powerful expression of religious experiences. So, I believe and hold to my Christian faith and traditions, the faith and traditions of my forbears. My faith provides a solid foundation for life; it buoys me up during the hard times, gives me a love for all humankind, and inspires a great joy in living.

3

The Faith of Believing

NURAH W. AMMAT'ULLAH
(ROSALIE P. JETER)

I am a woman of African descent who works as an archival librarian at the premier institute in the world for the documenting of the experiences and culture of people of African descent—The Schomburg Center for Research in Black Culture in New York City. I am a Muslim woman who chooses to wear *hijab*—head covering and modest dress—to comply with the Islamic tradition that women past puberty cover their hair and dress modestly in public spaces and in the presence of marriageable males. I am also the founder and executive director of the Muslim Women's Institute for Research and Development (MWIRD). All of these identities and their activities occur on the tightly woven fabric of Islam. I have embraced a different faith from the one I was socialized into in my early life. In my early childhood I was baptized Anglican and while growing up I enjoyed an eclectic religious education that included catechism, Pentecostal Bible School, Seventh-day Adventist youth group, and the feasts of the Yoruba-style indigenous religion of Trinidad—with the Shouter Baptists. Yet my faith has had great continuity and constancy. Uninterrupted throughout my life, I have had conversations with Allah, which began early in my childhood and have been a permanent source of comfort, awe, conviction, and motivation.

PUBLIC PRACTICE: GOOD WORKS AND KNOWLEDGE

In the Islamic tradition there are charges/instructions, documented in the revelation of the Qur'an and the subsequent text it has inspired, given to Muslims by Allah. Two of them are to do good works and to seek knowledge. For many of us these are often considered as exclusive entities. In my attempt to live a faithful life I aim to no longer separate these two acts of faith, arguing that in doing good works there is valuable knowledge to be had that will fortify our being as we continue on our journey of life. Indeed, all of our actions to educate ourselves and to be charitable in the world are understood as acts of faith and are important to the totality of being a practicing Muslim. To me, faith is an essential intangible that is as real and as necessary as the air that I breathe. My faith transcends the boundaries of my chosen religious tradition. My faith connects me to my grandmothers—though none of the immediate ones practice Islam—all of whom are devout practitioners of different faith traditions. What I share with each of them collectively is this "Real God" that is our own, the God of our familiar, who initiates, supports, sustains, confronts, and comforts our life journeys/paths of community building and acceptance as well as independence and defiance.

A practicing Muslim since my embrace of Islam, I strongly resonate with Allah's charge to Muslims to leave humanity better than we found it. I have sought ways to put my faith into action through the establishment of MWIRD. Founded in 1997, MWIRD is a non-profit multi-service organization facilitating networking, resource sharing, advocacy, scholarship, and research. We explore all matters and areas affecting the daily lives of women of faith, specifically Muslim women, with special focus on women who identify themselves as Western in culture. The organization's primary purpose is to provide infra-structural development through support services, training, and technical assistance program monitoring and to encourage interfaith dialogue among women of faith, along with research assistance to faith-based projects that are women centered.

Ultimately, MWIRD's mission is empowerment; it strives to enhance the quality of life for Muslim women in the West by coordinating, supporting, or creating services and tools from the Islamic body of knowledge. At the institute we work to address the transitional needs of new immigrants and the social-service needs of community members in neighborhoods of the southwest Bronx in New York City. These neighborhoods are the best examples of urban decay and governmental neglect. The work of MWIRD aims to provide services that lead to the empowerment of community members and stakeholders, while raising awareness of the creativity and genius of those living with and in institutionally created and systemic poverty.

Developed from our understanding and practice of good citizenship, our active response to basic human and social needs is coupled with an advocacy effort to help Islam and Muslims in the United States become a foundational part of the mosaic of ecclesiastic work, pastoral care, and faith-based community service in the general society. Through its programs and services MWIRD provides a platform for manifesting a multifaceted vision of practicing Muslim professional women who are Western in cultural and social identity and who hold a strong sense of moral and ethical responsibility for addressing and correcting local social and economic injustice. Our local response to human need is attached to our commitment to support and encourage women of faith in their efforts to research and study events and policies that affect our communities on all levels. It is our vision that more women of faith will become full participants in policy-making processes within our faith communities, the centers and institutions of civil society.

PUBLIC SPACE

The work of being the executive director of MWIRD places me in varied public spaces as an ambassador, a spokesperson on behalf of segments of the Muslim community, especially Muslim women, and other women of faith. These spaces of interaction are often secular, and at times I have even experienced them as anti-Islamic and antireligious. Every public appearance with my *hijab* makes me externally identifiably Muslim and subject to all of this society's sentiments, biases, and ignorance about my chosen faith and the people who adhere to it. Sadly, some of these biases even come from within the Islamic community. My *hijab* has allowed me to remove my body from public display, and it has forced my human interactions to be premised in an arena other than the physical; I now experience the exterior of my body as sacred. The *hijab* gives me ownership of my body; I decide who I share it with and how I share it. This I experience as empowerment. The external *hijab* helps one develop the more valued *hijab*, the internal one—the *hijab* of the heart—which is strived for by men and women with equal passion because it is believed to place one closer to Allah/God.

However, I would strongly caution that the *hijab* and the choice to wear it not be taken as indicators of devoutness or religiosity. In the *hijab* we find the paradox of liberation and oppression. Many Muslim women scholars like Amina Wadud and Ingrid Mattson, both North Americans, provide insight and clarity on this subject that I have found to be useful—you may benefit from their ideas as well. I will not provide citations, hoping that if you have not already done so, you will begin educating your mind and heart by searching for good reading material. Life as I have experienced it most often has placed me on the fringes of the social, cultural, and political contexts that I must navigate daily. My marginal existence paired with my conversations with Allah/God generates a life lived with the knowledge that there is an unseen hand of benevolence shaping the events of my life. I have had many accomplishments, gifts, and joys in life—some tangible and some not. For example, international travel has been as rewarding as my homeland experiencing the diversity of West Africa in the Bronx, where I am welcomed into the many small ethnic communities from that region. It is a joy to me that MWIRD serves in the Bronx, New York City—as joyful as being able to enjoy a sunset on the shores of the Dead Sea. All of these events have filled me with awe in the unexpectedness and perfection of each experience.

These good experiences were always exactly what I needed at the time, even when I was not always aware of my need. I still believe because I am still living; I would not be able to live without my faith. There is so much I do not know, cannot know, that my developing faith allows me to be okay with not knowing as a temporary place until I have been educated and made more fully aware of the eternal truths

PUBLIC ACTIVISM

I was scared by the level of poverty and disconnectedness from the society in which the community I joined when I first moved to the United States lives. My fear drove me to act on my faith by participating in community efforts at the church I attended; it marked the birth of my spiritual activism in the United States. I say spiritual as opposed to religious because even after the embrace of another faith tradition, my spiritual activism continued and is still present many years into my embrace of Islam. Nowhere in my life is this point of speaking the truth and finding the divine attributes in the other expressed more accurately than with the work that MWIRD does at the food pantry in the Bronx. The majority of persons we serve at the food pantry have lived in the United States for less than ten years. Our clients are primarily women who do not speak English and who have little or no social capital in the environment that is now home—the Bronx, New York City. We serve all who express a need for emergency food and hunger relief regardless of religious affiliation; most of the persons we serve are not Muslims. My obligations as a Muslim are to welcome the traveler, feed the hungry, and be compassionate to the indigent. When combined with the American cultural values and practices of welcoming the immigrant, our Muslim-American values allow us at MWIRD to extend the love and hospitality of Islam at our tent in the Bronx—the food pantry.

While we at MWIRD and others like us do not demand changes in which the other becomes us, we use our spiritual activism and knowledge to seek and agitate for intra-faith and interfaith changes that lead to justice and equality for all. The fellow travelers on this path act as the benchmark of my own spiritual activism. They have set the bar, which I now attempt to attain. Likewise, I am a role model for them, and they see MWIRD as a worthy example.

How does one discuss faith and one's understanding and application of it in one's life? I tend to think of faith and practice this way: Like the human senses, there are very complex theories about the mechanics of faith, how faith works, and a common understanding that it may not work in the same way for each person. Though we have some general knowledge of how our bodies work in regard to our senses, I do not believe that individuals spend much time thinking about how our senses work or how our faith works. We know that our senses, which are operational, work and are most times on automatic or reflex use. My faith is very much like another sense—it is there, it is drawn on by reflex, it happens while everything else is happening in my life. Like my other senses, the ways in which I receive, understand, or recall the messages and instructions of my faith are often not conscious.

There is a parallel dimension to this intuitive, reflexive, and unconscious faith, one that is studied and intentional. I call this an educated faith. Educated faith calls Muslims to seek knowledge from the cradle to the grave, a saying attributed to the Prophet Muhammad (peace and blessings be upon him). It should be noted that there are no gender restrictions on this call, like the pillars of Islam, meaning that it is applicable to all—male and female. Islam in its teachings and early history mandated, encouraged, and supported the scholarship and education of women in matters of religion and civil society, including public administration, governance, and social welfare and service. From the advent of the prophethood of Muhammad (peace and blessings be upon him) through to present times, there have been women across cultures who became public figures because they acted on their knowledge and faith. I am therefore one of many.

Faith, a necessary intangible of my life, is a tool. I am convinced that faith has opened many doors for me and those that I serve. It is a tool without which I would not be here. My faith has answered so much of the unexplainable while allowing an openness of mind and heart enabling me as I travel the earth to embrace and be embraced by many. My faith has allowed me to be in awe of the deep faith passion of illiterate and poor persons who practice many literature-based faith traditions. From my experiences I make a very strong argument that faith is not only about texts or literacy. Faith needs to be reconsidered as the manifestation of another way of knowing. My faith permits me to feel grateful for the simplicity of the divine beauty that is a central component of all that exists.

I am truly grateful for being able to experience this beauty, which then strengthens and expands my faith. As a person responsible for founding and currently operating a faith-based human-service community organization, these issues of believing and belonging are always present as potential religious, political, and ideological battlegrounds. To diffuse tension and turn battlegrounds into grounds for building centers for a peaceful housing for our shared hopes and dreams, we need to learn how to appreciate, encourage, and support one another. A main aim of the organization I founded is to demonstrate the precedent of Islam that teaches that Muslims are the vice-regents of Allah with the responsibilities to be care-givers to all of creation. Staying true to this vision has required transcending intra-faith and inter-faith boundaries. The reward has been to create a holy mission pleasing to Allah in the service of a small portion of humanity as we seek the mercy of Allah/God. What a joy!

PART II

The Rewards of Belonging

4

A Matter of Belonging

VANESSA L. OCHS

For me, as an observing Jew, believing is not about having certainty about God or being in a relationship with God. It is about belonging, not just to a people, or even to a culture, but to one particular embodied, artistic, noble way of being human. Had I been born into a Chinese Buddhist family, given my personality and my sensibilities, I imagine I would have embraced and championed my heritage. Had I been born into an Irish or Italian Catholic family, I am sure I would have become a nun, if that were the most intense way I could live out my belonging.

What I believe is that I belong to Judaism, and that my belonging determines, in good part, what I am supposed to do, act, feel, support, cherish, and even imagine.

A former religious studies major comes to speak with me. She comes from a Jewish family, and during college, she had taken on several Jewish religious practices, such as keeping kosher and observing the Sabbath, that she had never observed at home. Now, with tears in her eyes, she confesses that she has concluded that Judaism, the whole kit and caboodle, may not be "true" and hence is possibly not worth practicing. By "not true" she means three things: (1) that the Bible may not be factual; (2) that the history of the Jewish people that she has read may have been constructed to promote and support different ideologies; and (3) that there may not be a God. I am embarrassed that after having studied in my department for four years, she persists in measuring religion—at least her own religion—according to such naive standards of what she calls truth.

I ask her, "Is the play 'King Lear' true?"

She says, "No."

I then ask, "Does that make it less compelling as a piece of art, less illuminating, less important for actors to train their whole lives to be able to perform it well?"

She says, "No."

47

"It's the same with religion," I tell her. "When a religion is compelling, illuminating, or a source of organization and structure for one's whole life, it doesn't need to fit narrow definitions of truth. When a religion gives you and your community meaning and identity, it is *real*, in the same way a work of art is real. What you believe in is its realness, not its truth."

As "real" as Judaism has been for me it has never been ideal. Fortunately, in my lifetime, Judaism has undergone dramatic feminist transformation. This process of change was initiated in the 1970s by women a few years older than I, such as Paula Hyman and Judith Plaskow. At that time my own misgivings about women's place in Judaism were coming to a boil, but I was not yet able to articulate them for myself. The possibility of change was in the air, and pioneer Jewish feminist-scholar-activists were putting themselves on the line to lobby for a place for women in the rabbinate and in the field of Jewish studies. I eventually found my own ways to contribute to the process of bringing feminist insights and women's experiences into Judaism. I have worked with the Women of the Wall (a group of Jewish women who have engaged in a long legal struggle for the right to pray aloud together, wear ritual garments, and read from the Torah scroll at the Western Wall in Jerusalem). I have been able to encourage Jewish women to study the Talmud (which had long been the province of Jewish men), to create new rituals marking the events in women's lives, and to mentor young women planning to become rabbis or beginning their rabbinic careers. Surely, I could not have resigned myself to praying only in the women's balcony, to studying only the limited range of sacred texts once permitted to women, or to belonging to a religious community that was disgusted or amused by the thought of women as public spiritual leaders. Had there been no context for me to register my own misgivings and eventually make my own spiritual contributions, my feeling of disenfranchisement and despair might have easily overshadowed the pleasures I had in belonging. Familiarity, memory, and community could not have trumped anger, disappointment, or humiliation.

Judaism has long had the capacity to renew itself—that is, I believe, its vibrancy. There is a reason this group has survived multiple destructions of its most sacred places, exiles, and attempts at annihilation. It is functionally a community based on biology (one inherits identity as a Jew through a parent), but in important ways it is a community based on one's capacity to imagine oneself back into time and across space. "I make this covenant, with its sanction, not with you alone, but with those who are standing here with us this day before the Lord our God and with those who are not here this day." Rashi, the medieval commentator, taught that these verses (Dt 29:13–14) move us to understand that the covenantal community includes not just those who literally stood at Sinai but "all the future generations." That is, Jews can, through an act of imagination, defy the boundaries of time and place and still hear the voice of revelation spoken at Mount Sinai.

I believe Jews are still part of a community that hears God's voice and adheres to sacred ways of being human together. We can hear the echoes of the divine voice that originated in antiquity, and we must listen to the divine voice we ourselves are hearing right now. As a good postmodernist, I have no trouble believing that we can sustain multi-vocal, even contradictory hearings.

A Christian college freshman, a friend of my daughter's, originally from Korea is a guest at our house for Sabbath dinner. She interrogates me about my belief in God. "What is your relationship to God?" she asks while we are still on the soup course, and before I can even formulate an answer, she wants to know if Jews believe God is good, and while I am at it, how do Jews understand why there is evil in the world? I tell her that from my perspective, she is asking the wrong questions if she wants to know how this particular Jew who sits in before her thinks.

I say, "You come from Korea, and Korea was once your whole world. You spoke the language of Korea, and ate its foods, and the gossip of your neighborhood in Korea was what mattered. When you think of beauty and of home, it's the slide show of Korean landscapes that flashes in your memory." I told her that Judaism, for me, is like that. It's about coming from a particular world that is all enveloping and has nearly everything in it that makes you feel loved. It helps you to make sense and provides answers (whether or not they satisfy you) for small questions, such as "What's for dinner?" and for big questions, like "What qualities should I look for in a spouse?" Most Jews, if you ask them, can tell you what Jews are supposed to believe. Monotheism, they might tell you, and following that, perhaps the Ten Commandments. Beyond that, they tend to leave the "What do Jews believe?" question to rabbis and theologians. In the back of their heads, they may have decided that not knowing the answers, but imagining that someone else might know, is sufficient. They may even have decided that they do not believe in God at all, or do not accept that God controls the unraveling of the good and evil that transpires in the world. This lack of belief does not make a dent on their Jewish belonging. I told our dinner guest, "For many Jews, Jewishness is about identity, and not about truth-claims."

When I went to graduate school to study anthropology of religion, I was trained to critique those professors of religion who taught their classes: "These are the three key beliefs of X religion: monotheism, a belief in an afterlife, and the existence of original sin." I was taught to shun those who expected their students to memorize these truth-claims and spout them back on exams, as if knowing those generalizations, which might have little to do with how people in those faith traditions experience living out their faiths, counted for really knowing that religion.

I was taught something I knew in my gut: in most of the world, people do not "do" religion only on special moments of their life. Religion is not a way of being that gets activated on Sundays, holidays, or at big rites of passage. Religion is the whole of life for most people, all of who they are, the lens through which everything is experienced. Colleen McDannell refined this insight, leading me to abandon a previous assumption: that people of faith had beliefs, and through their rituals and practices they enacted them or embodied them. McDannell was suggesting what I had observed in myself and in other observing, religious people: with our lives, our things, our movements, our relationships and feelings, we are consonantly and creatively constructing a world that alternatively makes space for the sacred and blesses its presence. The doing and making don't follow the believing; they facilitate it, consulting back and forth with it. Or, doing and making simply don't rest on believing.

Previously, I had heard only one language for talking about religion, and it favored male creativity and male agendas. In that language, when you spoke about the beliefs of a religion, you were generally speaking about theology, doctrine, and rules. When you talked about ritual, you spoke about it as a manifestation of the ideas, and it was in this arena that women could participate as "worker ants," baking the breads for the holy meals, learning the steps for the sacred dance. They could act out what the men had codified. This was simply inaccurate.

When I was a teenager, I had a good many questions that rumbled through my head when I'd be trying to pray in synagogue: If I say the prayer in Hebrew and don't know what it means, is God still listening and understanding? If I say the prayer and do know what it means but don't have my heart in it, will God still be impressed by my showing up today? Does God really need all these psalms of praise, or does all the flattery sound offensive, particularly if it precedes a request? Will God still make peace and provide rain in its season if we don't ask? Should we see our unanswered prayers as a sign that God does not hear or cannot act? Now, when I go to synagogue, while I still recall my old litany of prayer issues, they are no longer the centerpiece of my worship practice, which I think of as "noticing and blessing."

I notice that a middle-aged couple, a second marriage for them both, has tiny twin girls, born through extensive IVF treatments, sitting in two little carriers between them. On either side of the parents are the grandparents—really, really elderly and wrinkled. I can tell the grandparents are pinching themselves. How many times had they given up the hope that they would be coming to a synagogue to name a grandchild? I notice that the grandmothers are both from suburban places, where women come to synagogue with their nails and hair done—wearing elegant suits and high heels. I calculate the extensive efforts the grandmothers had to engage in so they would look especially good for this day. The rabbi invites the family to come up front so the babies can be blessed. Other relatives I had not picked out emerge. These appear to be aunts and uncles, and they help the grandparents make their way up three steps, as if they are helping astronauts up a ladder into a spaceship. Once everyone is standing behind the table that holds the opened Torah scroll, the rabbi directs the new parents and all the relatives to recite, "Blessed are you, Lord our God, Ruler of the Universe, who has sustained us and brought us to this day." They are all crying and have a hard time getting through these words. I search in my own pocket for a tissue. Then the parents tell the story of how each baby got her first and middle names and her Hebrew name, and then they describe the exemplary lives of their namesakes. I have stopped noticing the grandmothers' fancy clothes. I feel the presence of these ancestors after whom the babies have been named. I think about how they can now live again through these wonder babies.

My noticing continues. Before the baby group even gets seated again, a new drama erupts. A member of the congregation will have an *aliyah*, a Torah honor, to mark her return from participating in a marathon with other women who are breast cancer survivors. She wants to say a special healing prayer for herself and the women she trained with. I am stunned by her courage and her openness and concern for others. While I do not think that God makes people better because they have friends and family who pray for them, I do imagine a long line of runners, and I see not only the breast cancer survivors but all the people whom I love whose health I worry about. I have a good hearty worry for them all and ask God to fix them up completely or, if that's not in the cards, to grant them as much happiness and comfort as a person can hold.

It's not over yet. A elderly man has returned from a trip to the place in Poland where his family perished in the Holocaust. He tells the rabbi he wants to come up to the Torah to *bentch gomel*, that is, to recite the blessing of thanksgiving said by someone who has come back from a harrowing or dangerous experience or journey. I know the man is not well-to-do, so saving up for this journey must have taken many years. "Such stories I could tell," he whispers so loudly to the rabbi that we can all hear, and I know I am not the only one reflecting on how the big story of Jewish history is unfolding here in our midst. He says his part of the blessing, and the congregants responds with, "May the one who has bestowed every kindness upon you in the past continue to bestow kindness upon you in the future."

God is here, I tell myself (but it's more a feeling than a thought), here in all these little dramas unfolding before us, each a ritual in which my fellow congregants have opened up their hearts and lives before us and before the Torah, and surely, before God. I experience God's presence in my capacity to merge my heart with that of the "stars" of the dramas and with my fellow congregants. That I can witness, empathize, and have the capacity to be so moved and feel compassion and gratitude is a blessing. Leon Wieseltier has put this state of spiritual attentiveness eloquently: "I am in a mind to bless. Blessed be the book, the page, the verse, the word. Blessed be the great names and the ungreat names. Blessed be the velvet that is the color of wine, and the wine. Blessed be the particle in the light and the light. Blessed be the shoulder and blessed be the burden. Blessed be the calendar. Blessed be the clock" (Wieseltier 2000, 754).

5

Confessions of a Jewish Feminist Atheist

JUDITH LORBER

A month before a dear friend of mine died, another friend in our network of Jewish feminists told me she said to the ill friend, "I'll pray for you, but you know I don't believe in God." I knew exactly what she meant by this paradoxical statement. I, too, don't believe in God, but right after my friend died, I went to my synagogue to say *kaddish*, the prayer for the dead. When another Jewish feminist friend died a month later, I went to Passover *yiskor* (memorial) services to say *kaddish* for both of them, and for my parents.

Kaddish doesn't mention death or the dead person being remembered—it only praises God. As an atheist who doesn't believe in an omniscient presence, what was I seeking at the synagogue? Comfort in ritual, comfort in community. I was not able to go to the funeral of either friend, and their families' memorial services for them took place several weeks later, so I sought more immediate comfort—and closure—in the synagogue.

Let me give you some biographical background for my Jewish identity and my feminist identity. I was a feminist first, a Jewish feminist later. Of course, I have always been a Jew, but I was quite disaffected for thirty years, from the age of fourteen when I knew I did not believe in God, to the time my son was seven, in 1974. My son knew he was Jewish but not what a Jew is. At that point I joined a synagogue to give him a Jewish education—and got one myself. I didn't "come back" to Judaism—I was superficially familiar with the rituals and the holidays but had no "learning"—no knowledge of the meaning of the liturgy or of the Torah, the center of Jewish theology. I knew Jewish history and the history of Israel but hadn't been to Israel. I had been more interested in comparative religion and, given my interest in art and travels in Europe, had been in more churches than synagogues. I could talk more about the Christian martyrs and Jesus' life than about the Jewish patriarchs and matriarchs.

MY JEWISH FEMINIST JOURNEY BEGINS

In the course of my son's six years of preparation for his bar mitzvah at the age of thirteen, I learned basic Judaism and basic Hebrew. I became active in the Reform synagogue I belonged to; it was in Greenwich Village and had a lot of people with my own liberal political views. In fact, I knew several from earlier days in politics. I did some proselytizing for introducing women biblical heroes to the Hebrew school curriculum and even became principal of the school for a year. But I was there more as a mother than as a feminist.

Meanwhile, the current feminist movement was burgeoning—this was the 1970s—and I was deeply involved in it, intellectually, politically, and professionally. As a feminist, I was developing courses for college students, doing research on women physicians, writing and publishing, and helping to organize a professional feminist organization, Sociologists for Women in Society. This was my home, my community.

At the same time that I was learning to be a Jew, Judaism was confronting feminism (see Levin 2000, 774–80). And so I started reading *Lilith,* the feminist Jewish women's magazine, and people like Judith Plaskow, author of the 1990 book *Standing Again at Sinai,* a plea for reinstating women into Judaism. I began to combine my Jewish life as a mother with my feminist professional and political life. I gave a talk at the synagogue on different types of Jewish feminism, and some like-minded women members and I wrote a feminist Sisterhood Shabbat. This shabbat combined the Jewish synagogue concept of sisterhood as the women's auxiliary with the feminist concept of sisterhood—both are, of course, communities of women.

I was aware of anti-Israel views among feminists and the disruptions at the United Nations conferences on women that Letty Cottin Pogrebin recently described (2003, 15–19), but I hadn't experienced them firsthand, so I didn't feel pulled between two important areas of identity and activism.

VISITING ISRAEL

I added Jewish feminists to my intellectual and friendship community. Many of them were Israeli, and I went to Israel several times. I lived in Tel Aviv and Jerusalem in 1992–93 on a Fulbright Award and taught at Bar Ilan University, one of the prestigious state universities organized for observant Jews. I was invited by my friend and sister feminist Dafna Nundi Izraeli to teach gender studies as a way of easing the comparatively conservative university into an acceptance of feminist-oriented scholarship and research programs similar to those already established at the more secular universities. Dafna subsequently established the Rachel and J. L. Gewurz Center for Research on Gender and the graduate program in gender studies at Bar Ilan

University. The Bar Ilan program is the only M.A./Ph.D. gender and women's studies program in Israel. She also endowed an annual Judith Lorber Lectureship in Gender and Society at Bar Ilan. I became quite well known in gender studies in Israel. My Judaism was taken for granted; my reputation was made on my feminist publications, lectures, and interchanges with gender scholars and students. My work meshed with the main feminist activities in Israel—a battle for gender equality.

While American Jewish feminists were struggling to change Jewish institutions, liturgy, and the rabbinate, Israeli feminists were more concerned with gender inequality in Israeli secular society—in the work place, the army, political life. Many of my Jewish Israeli friends were secular and attended religious services rarely; others were orthodox and accepted the separation of women from men in the synagogue and the male language of the liturgy and Torah. Neither group seemed as compelled as American Jewish feminists to change Jewish ritual; the battles were over gender equality in the professions, work organizations, and the military; marriage and divorce reform; and the issue of violence against women.

The feminist conferences I spoke at when I was in Israel included Israeli Arab and Palestinian women as well as observant Jewish women. Wigs and head scarves were both very much in evidence, but neither Judaism nor Islam as religions were ever a topic in these conferences on equality and identity politics. Identity politics were over national conflicts—Israeli Jew, Israeli Arab, Palestinian (Herzog 1999, 344–69)—or social status differences—European-origin Ashkenazi and North-African-origin Mizrachi (Dahan-Kalev 2001, 669–84).

Most of my feminist friends were members of the Israeli Feminist Network and peace organizations. Their goal was to achieve equality for all Jewish and Arab Israeli women, including those in ethnic minorities. Religion was not an arena for revolution. More criticism was addressed to Israel's masculinist stance that put security and defense before civil needs. The feminist focus was on gender reform of Israeli secular and civic society—advancing the position of women.*

Just to have tackled the issue of gender in the Hebrew language would have been nothing short of revolutionary. Hebrew is one of the most gendered of the world's languages; in order to say anything without indicating gender, you have to use neutral phrasing like "it may be said." An alternative is to feminize what you say or alternate the masculine and feminine—along the lines of *she and he, chairwoman and chairman.* You can't say *chairperson* in Hebrew, let alone refer to a gender-neutral God. You can say *ruah*—spirit, a feminine noun—instead of *melech*—king, a masculine noun. But feminizing god-language comes close to reinstating the Jewish goddess, Asherah (see Kien 2000; Patai 1990).

---

* A self-criticism among feminists was the elitism of affirmative action in Israel (see Izraeli 2003, 109–28).

MY ENCOUNTERS WITH U.S. FEMINIST JUDAIC SCHOLARSHIP

In contrast to the secular feminist activism and gender-oriented scholarship in Israel, Jewish feminists in the United States, writing in English, have developed gender-sensitive liturgies, women's rituals, and new interpretations of the Torah. Many of these women are Reform, Reconstructionist, and Conservative rabbis. In the thirty years that the colleges of these branches of Judaism have been ordaining women, their numbers have proliferated to the point where the non-Orthodox rabbinate has feminized.

The Jewish feminist exegeses of the Hebrew Bible, the Apocrypha, and the books of Samuel and Judges, as do the modern Christian feminist interpreters, pick up where Elizabeth Cady Stanton and other nineteenth-century feminists left off in *The Woman's Bible*. They all point out that the first creation story in Genesis tells us that God created humankind in God's image as male and female. They valorize Vashti, the rebellious queen in the book of Esther, and mourn the invisibility of Dinah, the sexually exploited daughter of Jacob and Leah. But the new interpreters go further, combining historical contexts and text analysis. Applying postmodern techniques, they literally read between the lines, looking at language, symbolic representations, and gaps in the text to come up with new readings.[*] Similarly, a search for Islamic rootedness and legitimation has led Islamist feminists to interpret the Qur'an from a woman's perspective (see Wadud 1999). These postmodern analyses of Judaic, Christian, and Islamic texts are all now part of my library.

CONTINUING MY JOURNEY

So to where have I come? My Jewish and feminist identities are now so interlocked that my next book (forthcoming from Norton) is called *Breaking the Bowls: Degendering and Feminist Change*. The title is a metaphor for a disruption in assumed values, a revolutionary change in thought, a paradigm shift. It is based on a translation of the colloquial Israeli Hebrew phrase *lo nishbor et ha-kelim*—a warning against "breaking the dishes" or making an irreparable breach by challenging accepted ideas and ways of doing things. This phrase has a kabbalistic background—during creation, ideal types of beings (angels) were contained in three bowls of light, and finite types of being (human beings) in six. As recounted in Gershom Scholem's 1965 book *On the Kabbalah and Its Symbolism,* the earthlings broke their six bowls, and their light was scattered. To me, breaking the bowls is a metaphor for the restructuring of thought and action—not just reforming

---

[*] See, among others, Bach 1999; Frankel 1998; Frymer-Kensky 2002; and Kates and Reimer 1994.

or resisting the old ways but rebelling against conventional thinking about gender and revolutionizing the gendered social order with imaginative ideas and radical practices.

Yet I would not call myself a Jewish feminist. Rather, I'm a feminist Jew—the distinction is that my feminism informs my Judaism, and my Judaism flavors my feminism. I am fascinated by the feminist interpretations of Torah because they are feminist and postmodern. As for ritual and institutionalized Judaism, as I said at the beginning, there I find community and comfort, but I want to see change there, too—more gender-neutral language in English, more use of the feminine in Hebrew, celebration of women prophets, innovative prayers that invoke the spirit of the universe instead of our sovereign or king. I would like Judaism to be a more inclusive religion, one that could encompass my Christian daughter-in-law and half-Jewish grandsons.

Like Emma Goldman, in my militant feminist mode I identify with Judith, who cut off the head of an enemy general and saved her community. In *Living My Life* Emma Goldman said, "At the age of eight I used to dream of becoming a Judith and visioned myself in the act of cutting off the head of Holofernes to avenge the wrongs of my people. But since I had become aware that social injustice is not confined to my own race, I had decided that there were too many heads for one Judith to cut off."

But in my gender theory mode, I turn to Miriam, a prophet and leader in the desert, who danced with the women at the shore of the Red Sea after the Israelites' safe passage, and, it is said in kabbalah, "by making a circle dance, she drew down the supernal light [from the source] where the categories of masculine and feminine do not exist."

6

A Woman, a Christian, and an Academician

RHONDA HUSTEDT JACOBSEN

I am a woman, a Christian, and an academician. More pointedly, I am a woman who is both a feminist and a contented wife and mother. An active and devout Protestant Christian who considers herself both an evangelical and a liberal, I am an academician who is both a faculty member (professor of psychology) and a college administrator (director of faculty development). In short, my life is lived at the intersection of a number of supposedly oppositional roles and/or concerns. What is perhaps most odd is that I am at ease at these points of intersection. Rather than feeling pulled apart by what others might see as a series of unmanageable tensions, I (perhaps naively) experience my life as a relatively balanced and coherent whole. I like being a woman, I feel enriched by my Christian faith, and I thrive as an academician. In terms of the title of this book, I am not merely "still believing" after all these years, I am joyfully believing, although in slightly different ways and for more articulate reasons than I did ten, or twenty, or thirty years ago.

This means that my experience may not be at all typical. Perhaps I am an oddity, off the bell curve, out in the region where normal character types never wander. But maybe I am more average than first appears. Maybe many women—many intelligent, religious women—live lives fairly similar to mine. I actually think that is the case, and I hope my story helps illumine theirs. There is no necessity to live at one end or another of anyone else's bipolar view of the world.

To say I am perfectly content with my complexly overlapped experience of life may be a bit of an overstatement. Life is not always easy. On average, women still do not earn the same wages as men regardless of how educated they are, and sometimes I have seen that fact reflected in my own paychecks. In many Christian circles women are still considered second-class members of their communities of faith (a sad fact that is also true of most other faiths), and from time to time I feel that prejudice directed at me. Finally, the academy is a place where the too ready admission of personal faith can cause one to be marginalized, and I have sometimes seen that played out in front of me. So things are not always daisies and blue skies. But I prefer to see life as half full rather than half empty. I very much enjoy my work, and most days I am amazed anybody is willing to pay me to do what I so enjoy doing. Women are treated as full equals with men in my immediate Christian circles. In my life as an academician I have rarely felt any negative judgment against me because of my faith. It is also important to remember that life is not easy for anyone. We all have challenges to face and obstacles to overcome. So rather than dwell on the negative tensions that can exist among womanhood, faith, and the academy, I want to write mostly about what I see as the positive connections.

But let me be clear. I really do not see my life as exemplary. For the most part I did not consciously choose to be the person I have become, so I cannot take all that much credit for it. Of course there were choices along the way, but my life, like everyone else's, is also a matter of grace, serendipity, providence, and chance. So I will tell you my story as a way of illustrating a "still believing" life, not because my life is exemplary, but because it is the life I know best.

It may already be obvious that I am by training and intellectual disposition a psychologist—a counseling psychologist who knows that human beings are not rational machines and that the unfolding of one's life story is rarely if ever neat and tidy. People are dynamic entities. They are thinking, feeling, and active beings living side by side and in constant interaction with other thinking, feeling, and active human beings. Given those facts, it is practically tautological to say that life is unpredictable. Very few things are determined in advance. Still, the normal process of human development is not totally random, and psychologists describe the life span as a series of developmental stages. Some stage theories are overly rigid and unwarrantably dogmatic in the way they say human development has to take place, and I find such proposals both inaccurate as descriptions of actual human experience and intellectually stifling. However, a flexible and simplified notion of stages of human development does seem to make sense and does apply to most people. Erik Erikson in *Childhood and Society* describes life in terms of eight stages, each one characterized by a critical psychosocial task (Erikson 1963). The task of adolescence is to develop a sense of personal identity; the task of young adulthood is to establish intimacy in relationships; and the task of adulthood is generativity, a sense of contributing to the larger world. Although I am jettisoning Erikson's biologically based notion of gender, I will use those three stages to provide a framework to describe my own development and maturation relating to gender, faith, and intellectual inquiry.

Let me summarize where those developmental trajectories have pointed. With regard to gender, my self-understanding has changed very little over the years. Men and women are equal, and the socially constructed gender traits of masculinity and femininity seem to adhere to individuals largely without reference to their biological sex. I knew that as a kid, and I know that today. Where I have changed with regard to gender is more sociological: I am less tolerant than I used to be of social structures that stifle the full flourishing of women, even in those instances where women seem willing to accept externally imposed limitations for the sake of security and/or male companionship. With regard to faith, I grew up in an environment where one was told very clearly what one must think and what one must *never* do. (We were short on positive rules of Christian conduct.) Over the years I have come to alter those priorities, focusing on acting with integrity and thinking with authenticity rather than on believing every dogma and avoiding every possible church-defined sin. With regard to the academic life, I entered the academy more or less through the back door—I never planned to become a college professor—but I have more and more embraced this calling in life as my own.

GROWING UP: IDENTITY FORMATION

I grew up on a farm in Illinois—a very good place to grow up if you are a girl. Studies have shown that farm women are disproportionately represented among the ranks of women who have become public leaders in American society (Van Leeuwen 1990). Perhaps this is because growing up on a farm makes it so evident that gender is constructed. In an odd way gender roles were both idealized and undercut on the farm, at least on my farm. Like my brothers, I would grab a shovel and gleefully swat the rats that ran out of the corn crib during shelling—competing to see who dispatched the most. Gender didn't matter. But when it came to ordinary chores I got assigned all the indoor housework, while my brothers worked outdoors doing boy stuff. Gender did matter. When I was ten, I was old enough to drive the pickup truck down the road and out in the fields to deliver lunch or needed equipment to my dad and his crew during harvest. Gender didn't matter. But as a sixteen-year-old licensed driver, with expectations that my dad would buy me an old used car as he had done for my brothers, I was told girls didn't need cars because they were supposed to get boyfriends to drive them around. Gender definitely did matter. The not very subtle lesson I learned from this was not that I should be a good traditional young lady (though I did oblige by finding boyfriends who could get me off the farm), but rather that gender roles are largely arbitrary. They can be invoked as rules of conduct by those in power, but there is nothing natural or necessary about most of them.

It was not just growing up on the farm that taught me this, it was growing up with my own two unique, intelligent, and complex parents, neither of whom fit the standard stereotypes of the mid-twentieth century. My mother was a college graduate and a middle-school teacher in our hometown. She is one of the most competent, rational, and hard-working human beings I have ever known. While she undoubtedly would have considered herself a good, submissive wife, she was the one who set the standards that ran our home. No one would have ever questioned that. She knew her mind and knew how to get things done. Her faith contributed to that. Mom had been raised in the Swedish section of Rockford, Illinois, where her parents, aunts, and uncles had developed their own peculiar theology and started their own small church (called simply "the class") while she was a kid. She knew what real religion was, and even though she had become a Baptist ("the class" had rejected the ritual of baptism, and my brothers and I were cautioned never to mention baptism when my grandparents were around) she maintained a strong sense of religious orthodoxy. My mother knew exactly what to believe and precisely what not to do, and that package of faith was communicated very effectively to her children.

My father was cast out of a very different mold. He was very smart—gifted enough to win a full college scholarship based on standardized testing in eighth grade. But he never attended college, dropping out in ninth grade to work the family farm during World War II. Dad was a bundle of contradictions. He was by far the more sensitive and compassionate of my two parents, but he also had an awful temper. He was a man's man who loved nothing more than fishing, hunting, and running a trap line, but he also wrote poetry. He was a gifted farmer and community leader (president of the local school board), but he never much enjoyed being around crowds of people. He was also a Lutheran—at least he was before he married my mom—a dancing, beer-drinking, fun-loving Lutheran. When he fell in love with my mom he agreed to become a Baptist—and he really did try to become one—but he never seemed able to pull it off with enough conviction and consistency to satisfy my mother. In family arguments her trump was to call my father an unregenerate Lutheran pagan, and his retort was that she was a pious Baptist hypocrite.

Growing up in my family, I knew there were different ways of being Christian—better and worse ways, and sometimes just alternative ways. That knowledge has helped me wade through the positive and negative dimensions of faith that are typically wound tightly around each other in people's lives. Whether they intended to or not, my parents taught me not to expect people to be saints—not even the best of Christians—and that has inured me to the tendency to reject faith because some (or most) Christians don't live up to their own highest ideals.

It is no wonder that when I went to college I gravitated almost immediately to the study of psychology. My parents advised me to get a certificate in teaching—"a girl's insurance policy," they called it—so I could get a decent job after college if I couldn't find a good man to marry. I took their advice, being the practical-minded farmer's daughter that I am, but I chaffed at the underlying presuppositions. I did well in college partly because I had always been a good student, but also partly because I had learned how to balance work, study, and play from watching my mother. Perhaps it would be more accurate to say I actually had a great time in college, which included among other things being a cheerleader for the football and basketball teams. Traditional gender roles can be fun. But then, in my last year at school, I took a social science seminar course with S. Richey Kamm, a wise white-haired political philosopher, thinker, and unbelievably gifted teacher. One day Professor Kamm called me to his office and asked a question that changed my life: Given that God had blessed me with a fine mind, what was I planning to do with it? It was the day when I began to consider a life characterized by intentional thinking.

YOUNG ADULTHOOD:
INTIMACY, CAREER, AND MATURING CONVICTIONS

Jake and I had been friends in college but never really dated. After working together for a summer in Europe, he asked me to marry him before we had an official first date. The surprise is that I said yes. In many ways nothing much changed in my life. Jake had been planning to attend Yale Divinity School, but he switched to the University of Chicago and we rented an apartment in my small Illinois hometown where I was a counselor in the local high school. From the beginning Jake never treated me as anything less than a full human being, and I treated him in the same way. In an era when many of our friends were trying to hammer out detailed egalitarian marriage contracts (I'll wash dishes on Mondays, Wednesdays, and Fridays, and you get them the other days; I'll dust and you vacuum) we seemed to fall easily into a natural pattern of making decisions together and sharing chores more or less evenly. Even after we had kids (which happened a lot sooner than planned), we continued to enjoy an easy mutuality in our family life and decision-making despite the added complexity that children bring to a marriage. This arrangement was part choice but also part serendipity. We fit together well. Gender was not an issue.

But our church—my old Baptist church, where I was still a member—had problems understanding our kind of marriage. One assistant pastor in particular (a fellow whose older brother was a well-known evangelical champion of male leadership in church and society) took umbrage at our egalitarian relationship. In a public meeting one Sunday morning he asserted that if I did not learn to submit to Jake and let him be the decision-making head of our home, our marriage would soon end in divorce. Perhaps needless to say, we left that church shortly thereafter. We didn't leave in a huff. What would have been the point? These were still my people in many ways, and I am not one to burn bridges. But clearly my old Baptist church had become a place where I could not flourish. This was never a matter of giving up on Christianity. I was simply no longer willing to settle for a sick or restrictive faith. God never intended women to be second-class human beings.

About the same time I experienced a similar transition with regard to my intellectual development. During my undergraduate years the field of psychology could roughly be divided into three camps. There were psychoanalytic theorists (Freudians), behaviorists (mostly followers of B. F. Skinner), and humanists (often attracted to the views of Carl Rogers). I never felt quite content identifying myself with one group or the other. With regard to counseling, I found the Rogerian style with its emphasis on listening the most natural fit given my own personality, but I could see that Freudians and behaviorists also made some good points. I adopted a fairly eclectic view, as different counseling strategies worked better or worse with individual people. I had never been much of a "joiner" in college—I preferred to move in and among many groups—nor was I much of an activist. Now I found I wasn't really capable of being an ideologue in my discipline either. Different schools of thought had their own strengths and weaknesses, and I wasn't ready to cling to one and reject all the others. At the time I would probably have described myself as wishy-washy. In retrospect, I think my decision to not take sides in this debate was an important step in making my thinking about psychology truly my own, and it has inured me to scholarly "sectarianism" ever since.

After my college years there was a general shift in psychology toward a new movement called cognitive psychology. One of the things common to psychoanalytic, behaviorist, and humanistic psychology was that human thought processes were either ignored or pushed to the margins of what was considered really important about human beings. That never seemed quite right to me. Thinking is important, and cognitive psychology validates that insight. So have I become a champion of the cognitive approach? Not really. While people are thinking creatures, they are also emotive beings and they are behavioral beings who are often locked into habitual patterns of action and reaction. Cognitive psychology provided the missing piece in what I see as a holistic conception of human personhood. We are thinking, feeling, and acting beings, and those three elements interact in our lives in complex ways. And then it dawned on me that what applies to psychology also applies to faith. Faith involves thinking, feeling, and acting, and mature faith seeks to balance those three elements in reasonable measure and constructive complementarity.

When Jake and I accepted teaching posts at Messiah College in Grantham, Pennsylvania, in 1984, we found ourselves by providence, choice, and chance in an environment where we both could flourish and where thinking, feeling, and acting were valued within the academic community we were joining and in the religious ethos that pervaded the campus. Messiah College is a church-related institution, founded by the Brethren in Christ Church, and the school takes its Christian identity as seriously as its commitment to academic excellence. Following the Brethren in Christ, Messiah College describes itself religiously as rooted in the Anabaptist and Pietistic Christian traditions. The Anabaptist movement began in the 1500s at the time of the Protestant Reformation and was characterized by its commitment to Christian ethics. Theological ideas were not ignored, but how a person lived was always considered more important than what he or she merely believed, and the key values of the movement were charity to all, mutual aid, and peace. The Pietistic movement began in the mid-1600s and focused on Christian experience more than on either beliefs or ethics. What was critical for Pietists was the personal dimension of faith: a lively sense of trust in God, humility in one's relations with others, gratitude for all we have received, and a sensitivity to the inner work of the Spirit in one's life.

This was a new mix for me—a new gestalt of intelligent and caring Christian faith. I found it, and find it, refreshing. It is perhaps necessary to say at this point that I am well aware that for some women, and for that matter for some men, the Anabaptist and Pietist traditions have been sources of great pain and frustration. When these traditions are not working well and are not living up to their own best ideals, they can be oppressive and destructive. But the same could be said of any and every religious tradition. My concern is more with how faith communities operate when they actually are living up to their ideals. When compared in that way, I find the Anabaptist and Pietist subtraditions within Christianity to be two of the most appealing options available. In this vision of faith what matters is the total orientation of one's life (not just getting all one's beliefs precisely defined and approved), and the goal is to help people toward full, rewarding, and peaceable lives. This vision also holistically values thinking, feeling, and doing, and, for me, that had already become a necessary component of any valid view of faith or human nature. I hadn't known fully what I was getting into when we moved to Messiah College (does anyone every really understand things like that in advance?), but what I found was a form of faith and style of scholarship that resonated deeply with the person I was already becoming. It has been a congenial place for me to teach and work ever since.

ADULTHOOD:
GENERATIVITY AND CREATIVE FIDELITY

At this point in my life a significant part of my academic energy is devoted to reflecting on the complex relations that exist between faith and learning. I teach at a school where the exploration of those connections is an explicit part of the curriculum. To a large degree this occurs in the senior seminar classes I teach (not unlike the one I took with Professor Kamm in my last year of college), where my students are required to take time to reflect on how their academic studies might require them to rethink certain aspects of their faith and how their faith might lead them to critique or reformulate some of the theories or practices that dominate their chosen field of study. Much of my work as director of faculty development focuses on the same topic, helping faculty members to become more articulate and self-reflective about the relationship of faith and learning (and vice versa) so they can better help their students think through those concerns. Thus a good deal of what I now do in my professional life is to help others understand ways to "keep believing," even while they are in the midst of being or becoming critical scholars in their disciplines.

One of the things I have found most helpful in this regard is to exchange the ideal of "living the answers of faith," a notion I inherited from my mother and her church, for the ideal of "living the questions of faith." I borrow that term from the Princeton University sociologist Robert Wuthnow. Wuthnow, in *Christianity in the Twenty-first Century,* argues that faith does not so much give believing scholars ready-made answers to the scholarly subjects they investigate as it gives them a different set of questions to bring to their work—questions of meaning, value, and responsibility, questions of origin and purpose, questions of pain and loss. These questions are not uniquely religious, but Wuthnow implies that believing scholars, compared to their more secular counterparts, may well find it harder to push those kinds of concerns aside. So when Wuthnow is asked how an intellectual can keep on believing, he answers that it is by "living the questions" of intelligent faith in dialogue with one's scholarly pursuits rather than by trying to provide neat and tidy answers to all the quandaries of life (Wuthnow 1993).

That kind of modesty and realism makes sense to me. Faith does make a difference in the way I see the world as a psychologist, but it does not tell me how to think. What faith provides is a series of very important hunches about how the world in general and people in particular are put together. Faith tells me that people are a mix of good and bad, and we shouldn't expect things to be otherwise. Faith tells me that people are interconnected— no one lives or dies by himself or herself—and thus they have responsibilities to one another. Faith tells me that all people have gifts and talents and that God wants them to use those gifts and talents to benefit those around them. Faith tells me that everyone is valuable, everyone deserves to be loved, and everyone really is special in God's sight.

The public face of religion in America—the public face of Christianity—is often one of uncaring dogmatism. Christians scream out their beliefs six inches away from the face of those they loathe as they picket an abortion clinic or protest the removal of the Ten Commandments from prominent display in the lobby of a state court building. Christian television preachers assure their viewers that God does not hear the prayers of Jews, or Muslims, or of anyone else who is not a true and orthodox Christian believer. Christian ministers command the women in their congregations to submit themselves to the headship of their husbands and to let the men run the church. Some Christians do these things, but not all.

If Christianity really was about all these negative things, it would be hard to keep on believing. But my understanding of Christianity is different. My understanding of Christianity is not about knowing exactly what everyone is supposed to believe. It is not about all the things people are not supposed to do. What Christianity is about is acting with love and integrity—about trying to live according to Jesus's teachings in the Sermon on the Mount—and it is about thinking as honestly as we can about this wonderful and complex world that God has made for us to inhabit. When I consider faith in that way, it is easy to keep on believing; in fact, it is impossible for me to envision doing anything else.

7

Priests Are Only Human, What Is Important Is God

ANNA KARPATHAKIS

I am envious of people who tell me that their spiritual journey has been an easy one. I am envious of two people who said to me, "Ask questions? It never occurred to me to question." I am envious of the student who said, "When I come across something that goes against my faith, I consider it as a test of my faith and arrange it properly in my mind." I am envious because my own faith has been riddled by questions, and I have not been able to arrange things properly in my mind. I am envious because my own spirituality has evolved in adversity—always in a social context, always in reflection of the politics of the day, always in the conversations I have with people, always in the details that make up our daily lives. Theology and belief have little meaning for me outside of social context, of the day-to-day events out of which our interpretations of theological texts occur.

If, as my maternal grandmother told me, "God is all around us, God is in the waters you swim in, the sun that dries you after you bathe, God is in us, in everything we do," then this trans-historical God's insistence on being contextualized and walking among the humble and not so humble of the earth, as far as I'm concerned, means that God is open to dialogue and questioning. And I, true to my Greek heritage, have over the years engaged God in too many dialogues. God, my grandmother would tell me, is in us, is a part of us, he is among us, in all we do. While man is not God, God became man and man returned to his original essence. And so, from a young age there was for me the idea that humanity derives from God, humanity is sacred, and all humans deserve the respect we give to God.

I must have been no more than six when, after questioning my grandmother about why my aunt's only baby died, she said, "It would be better to believe without questioning. But remember, if you must question, just know that God looks inside the heart of everyone and knows exactly what is there." For me, that was a go-ahead to ask questions. For if God did see in my heart, he would see questions that were at the very least baffling for a young child and later on for a grown woman. I remember my grandmother beginning her prayers late on Friday nights, ending work early on Saturdays to attend vesper services, and waking early the next morning to attend Sunday services. Being aware of the meaninglessness of hyperboles, I will nevertheless use one: my grandmother was the most religious person I have met in my life. She was a godly woman. For her, God was real, his mercy and wrath equally powerful. For my grandmother, God was to be learned about in both the Old and the New Testaments. Her nightly reading consisted of these texts. By the age of ten I knew of Jesus' life and miracles, the religious calendar, day by day, the saints and their deeds, the symbolism of the holidays throughout the year.

As I snuggled up next to my grandmother each evening, she would read verses of the Old and the New Testaments to me, in biblical Greek, asking me questions along the way. What did the wine mean? And the fish? Who was Lazarus, and why is his day celebrated during the Easter month? Why did Jesus take the time to bring a total stranger back to life? Could I also at least help those I love through my own faith and love? For if we are all sacred and loved equally by God, then what does it mean for a mere child to facilitate that which God intended for his children? And what of being "saved"? We are all saved; we are all intended to join God in heaven when our time on this earth ended. God, she told me every night, loves all his children equally. She would tell me stories of Jesus' childhood, her own childhood, her siblings, her mother and her aunts, her father and her uncles, when they were children, living on the margins of the Ottoman Empire, and how their faith in God and trust in their priests sustained them. Invariably, by the end of the night she would whisper in my ear, "God loves you and God is good. May God keep you safe in your journeys tonight and bring you back to me in the morning." Alas, I am no longer ten. I have selectively emptied my mind of the religious calendar and the saints, but I still hold on to the prayer I myself often repeat with my own child.

A few months ago I vented my frustration with my initial attempts to write a paper entitled "Do I Believe or Do I Belong?" to my niece. I said, "I suppose I could make a snappy remark such as 'a little of both, a little of neither, or a lot of both and a lot neither.' I have the luxury of making such snappy remarks and not fear ostracism from my God or from my group, because as a member of an ethno-confessional group, I was born with a God and shall die with a God. The only way to lose this God is to convert to another religion. Turning away or simply not attending church is not enough. And the truth is that as a Greek immigrant woman, American by citizenship, living in New York City in the early part of the twenty-first century, I am not going to denounce my group or my God. Certainly not when so many white Americans are scrambling to get into my religious community."

My niece rolled her eyes and muttered, "Oh, God. All right, I don't want to know your theory on whites and the church; let's leave that for later. First, are you religious?" Without a loss for words, so characteristic of fools, I quickly retorted, "Yes. No. Yes. No. It depends what you mean by religious."

She proceeded to lay out the basic criteria of religiosity. "Do you attend church on a regular basis?"

"If by regular you mean regular intervals, yes I do. Holy Thursday or Good Friday and Panayia [the Dormition of Mary, on August 15], if I'm in Greece."

"I mean often. Do you believe in Jesus?"

I ask, "Jesus as God or the symbolism of Jesus? Are the faith cops here?"

"But you believe in Panayia," she said, "as the bearer of life, and the sanctity of Jesus as a child. Wait a minute. Didn't you say that the church sees Panayia as a vehicle that God used to create his son?"

I laughed. I assumed she heard the same sermon I had heard years earlier given by a male priest. We have only male priests, and so all of the questions that women have in the church are answered by male priests according to the Church Fathers' writings—something I myself had been reminded of by a couple of priests back in the days when I was foolish enough to engage priests in questions and discussions. Obviously, I was not the only one doing such things. Two young women had asked the priest about the importance of Mary, Panayia, as the bearer of God, and the priest felt obliged to set things straight. "God," we were told one Sunday morning, "used Mary as a vehicle through which to produce Jesus, the man-God." Many years later I read this very argument in a paper that a priest/theologian delivered to a convention of the Eastern Orthodox faithful. I wrote a review of the volume in which this article was published. Many years later an older woman friend repeated the words she has so often shared with her closest friends throughout the years: "Women are the creators of life. Priests are not. God is life and God chose Panayia to create life." More recently, the same woman friend added, "We have Panayia, and before Panayia we had Athena."

Different family members often remind me that "there are questions you simply do not ask because they lead nowhere or simply have no answers." I, of course, very often fight back with, as I did quite recently:

> This is not the Greek way. Greeks always ask questions; we're supposed to. You think that many Greeks believe in Panayia's virginity? There's a difference between the symbolism and the literal interpretation of the Bible. Like I said, are the faith cops out? Because faith cops exist only in the *American* Greek Orthodox Church, not in the *Greek* Greek Orthodox Church. Careful, 'cause a lot of the things you value about women's freedoms are seen as sin and heresy by these new faith cops.

The new faith cops are the converts to our church, the Americans who use knowledge of history and understanding of symbols, canon law, and depth of belief as litmus tests of religiosity. The church, they argue, should be managed by the true faithful, not simply by Greeks who happen to be Orthodox from birth.

I look at some of the women around me, strong women, feminists in action, although perhaps not in terms of formal ideology, and wonder why and how they could put aside or overlook issues they hold so dear regarding women's lives and rights to determine their own destinies and be willing to kiss a priest's hand to show respect.

It is often difficult for those not born into a church to understand the contradictions that those of us born into ethno-confessional groups or into a church must face. Two or three friends have over the years invited me to attend their places of worship. These are, of course, not the Greek Orthodox Church. I cannot attend other churches or places of worship without running the risk of denying my group's history, my history, my son's history. The family of my husband, as refugees from Asia Minor and by extension my son's family's history, has been greatly affected by its ethnicity and religion. My son's grandfather was born on the side of the road as his parents were fleeing the Kemal Attaturk's Young Turks. The grandfather of my son's grandmother was slaughtered before the eyes of her father, at the time only four. When the Turkish soldiers asked the child where his father was hiding, the child pointed to the haystack into which the man had fled. And then her mother's story, her father's story as an adult man, her story, her husband's and his family's, my son's father's history—all are tied to our being an ethno-confessional group.

My paternal grandmother's best friend was a Turkish woman living next door to her on the island of Rhodes. Living on a smaller nearby island a couple of decades after the Dodecanese had formally joined Greece, I had never encountered Turkish soldiers, simply the history of the War of Independence as taught to us by our teachers during the military dictatorship. One day I asked my paternal grandmother if she was afraid of Turks. She blew out hard. "Such nonsense," she quickly muttered. She paused. She then added that when she was a little girl, she had heard of fighting between Greeks and Turks on the island of Crete. A few weeks later a group of Turkish young men, who looked as though they could have been soldiers, had visited her neighborhood. It was the only time she had ever felt scared in the presence of Turks. She feared the knife and gun one of the young men had on his belt. I remember her shaking her head, whispering, "I'm an old woman, and I still don't understand." She said that her Turkish neighbors never bothered her, they were good people. Then there was the fighting and the killing. Mothers on both sides, she said, crying for their sons. "Why?" I think I remember the words, "Our blood is red no matter who the God we pray to or the leaders we follow."

My mother tells me stories of when she was a teenager and would go to church and pray that the Italians, and later the Nazis, would leave the island. The Greek Orthodox Church, I proudly announce to my Jewish friends, holds a unique place and honor during World War II, since it was the only church in Europe that did not legitimate or turn a blind eye to Hitler's holocaust of the Jews.

Religion is politics, and for Greeks, in our relations with other nation-states and ethno-confessional groups neighboring us, religion has been a brutal form of politics. To convert to another religion would mean denouncing and giving up my son's history. As the mother and thereby the one responsible for my family's spirituality and religious and ethnic identity, I cannot make this break in history. Such a break would mean that my son would lose the opportunity to learn the important lessons daily cultivated from this history. And yet, I have not yet been able to answer the ethical and moral dilemmas that arise from these histories. My grandmothers' humanism arose at a time when war was commonplace. My paternal grandmother's lifelong friendship with a Turkish woman demands peaceful negotiations and coexistence. My husband's family's history as refugees from Asia Minor is the background against which my son, through me, will eventually have to reflect upon and develop his own ethical system, hopefully an ethical system based on principles of peace and respect. For, as my paternal grandmother said, "our blood is red, no matter who the God we pray to."

Ours is a history of the oppressed still threatened by a more powerful nation-state refusing to give up its legacy as the inheritor of the Ottoman Empire and which, from its perspective, has wrongfully been robbed of its authority to rule over other groups in the region. Ours is also a history of the oppressor. Our church, which was instrumental in our survival as a group under Ottoman occupation (and later the British, French, Italian and Nazi occupations) now has its own nation-state. Social ideologies and politics in my church, as in all other religious institutions, are consecrated as part of the theology. The Greek far right has in the past forty years been using this God to create politics of exclusion. The recent Albanian immigrants to Greece are mistrusted, often because the Albanians collaborated first with the Ottomans and later with Nazis. The Church of Greece is constructing an ideology and identity of Hellenic Orthodoxy and has been at the forefront of stirring up nationalist fervor and Muslim phobia with the numerous wars in the Balkans between the Orthodox and the Muslims. It lobbied hard to maintain religious identity information on identification cards in Greece. This, according to the church and those on the right, is the only way to distinguish between Greeks and immigrants, between the true Greeks and the non-Greeks who live in the country.

In the United States the Greek Orthodox Church has been riddled with its own identity and other political conflicts. The politics on all levels of the church reflect the politics of the three societies the church comes into contact with on a daily basis: the United States, Greece, and Turkey. The church in the United States was created by working-class immigrants. When I first came upon the Orthodox Christian Laity (O.C.L.), I think I took in a deep fresh breath. "Ah," I remember thinking to myself, "people interested in removing the church from nationalist politics." My euphoria was short-lived, as I soon discovered that nationalist politics was simply taking a 360 degree turn to ethno-racial politics and contextualizing the church within the American social and political framework and ideologies. The descendants of the earlier immigrant cohorts have for the past three decades been competing with the post-1965 immigrants for control of the local parishes and the archdiocese itself. The Americanizers want to redefine the church from being immigrant and ethnic to being American and pan-ethnic, that is to say, a "white" church. At this point the immigrants are standing in their way of molding a religious institution in ways that reflect their social and professional achievements. While one priest I interviewed decried his parishioners' ostracism of an African American family, another commented with pride that "Greeks have become American." He added that when he was a child, he would look out at those gathered in the church and note that they were "dark." "Now," he said, "they're lighter. We are Americans." A friend recently asked, "But why don't they just leave the church and create another church or join the Orthodox Church of America?" And the answer is, of course, that they can't, not without making a complete break with history, including their parents' histories as immigrants.

The Greek Orthodox are born with a God and in a church. Our baptism symbolizes our entry into the community of Christians and our worldly community. Ours is a historical and a "group God," who is also a personal God. Our God is a God of immense contradictions. He is a God of mercy and love. A God whose sense of justice can be interpreted by a child to be comparable to punishment, especially as this God is at times contextualized in current social relations and politics. Social ideologies in my church, as in all other religious institutions, are consecrated as part of the theology.

And so, while I, as a Greek, was born with a God and a church, I have spent the major part of my life running from both of them. My marathon, like other Greeks' and Greek Americans' marathons, began early on. When I was fifteen, on Holy Thursday of that year, my mother entered my room and told me that I was not to worship the icons that evening nor was I to receive holy communion on Saturday because I was menstruating. A few months earlier a priest had talked about homosexuality as a sin and, by extension, of homosexuals as sinners; I had heard my aunts talking about a man we knew, a kind man, being homosexual. The year before the priest warned parishioners against the threat of atheism and communism posed by a group of student activists handing out political leaflets outside the church. These students were presented as sinners who had lost their way. My own sister had been among the students handing out informational leaflets on the military dictatorship back home in Greece. In another sermon the priest told women to be obedient wives and daughters because the apostle Paul had said so.

I feared this God, who was strict with the people he supposedly created, with his children. I was confused. At the age of fifteen I wondered why God would create me in a lesser image of himself, unlike my brothers, who were created in his image. My cousin, who was seventeen at the time, argued with an aunt: "If God created me, then I too am a perfect creature like men. I am not dirty because I menstruate, this is part of nature, this is part of God's intent of reproduction." When the young women tried to engage older women in these discussions, the older women had no answers. What can you say to a seventeen year old who asks why God, the creator of the universe, would in effect put something so imperfect as a woman on this planet? And what about Eve, my cousin asked. Why is she vilified?

It was not until college that one of us learned that the apple in the Garden symbolized knowledge. When one of us learned this, the news spread like wildfire. We wondered if God could be supportive of a military dictatorship back home. We wondered what God was going to do with homosexuals; would they forever burn in hell if they did not see the error of their way? Didn't my grandmother tell me that God's mercy and love for his creation was boundless? Don't our mothers love us even when we make mistakes? Does the father stop loving his child because the child does not act according to his wishes? And how do we know what the mother and father really intend if all we have is the writings of men who tell us that they knew first-hand of the mother's and father's wishes? Our priests told us that God loves us, but God also expected certain things from us. God's love, in other words, was conditional. And the conditions were set by the church fathers and re-cited to us by the male priests. When I was sixteen, my nineteen-year-old cousin pleaded with my aunt: "And how do you know that what the apostle Paul writes is what Jesus said? He's a man; of course he's going to say that women are to obey men."

Most of all, we kept asking, "Isn't a parent's love unconditional?" God was at times presented to us, or at least interpreted by many of us, as a mean God, a demanding God, a vengeful and wrathful God, a God who loved conditionally, and I, like so many of my cohort, did not want him. We would fight him. Or at the very least, we would reject him. When I was twenty, my brother (the only one of my siblings to show some sign of respect for the patriarchy of the church) said to me, "You think your morality is bigger and better than the priests'?"

I responded with a simple yes.

When I was seventeen, a woman announcer for one of the local Greek-language radio programs talked about a French sociologist's theory of religion. Religion and God he said, are created by people in a society; religion is the group's celebration of itself. I did not intuitively agree with the part of religion as a group's narrative and ideology. For me, as for so many of the young people of my generation, religion had been used to oppress and de-mean people. Women and homosexuals were being demeaned and devalued in the church. Religion, for me, had a repressive element that no other ideo-logical system I had till then experienced possessed. And so, I was overcome by a sense of freedom and empowerment against the priests who took free-doms in instructing me, my cousins, and my neighbors on how to live our lives. For, if God is only an ideology, then clearly I did not have to agree with him. Hearing of Durkheim's theory of religion at the age of seventeen, even if only in a format suited for the mass media, along with all the small lessons I had learned growing up in a politicized immigrant community, enabled me to understand the social origins of religion and furthermore, to distinguish between church and God.

In many ways, however, I went on to throw out the baby with the bath water. By the age of nineteen I had given up on the church. When my niece was six or seven, she commented, "You don't believe in God. Mommy does. Who is right?" A momentary revelation. I had been lucky enough to be raised in a church and a household that accorded me the freedom to reflect upon the religion, eventually to embrace it or reject it. My mother had done her job well in raising her children, introducing us to the church but acknowledging that ultimately any decision we made was our own. As an aunt, an older woman family member, I had the same responsibility now to my niece, to the next generation. I began attending church services on Good Friday and Holy Saturday, because, I thought, "everybody attends church these nights," and, "you can't do that to the child," my mother kept reminding me year after year after year. My niece, in her turn, had begun the new round of religious dialogues and questions in the family. She turned to her mother and grandmother for questions on theology and rituals, and to me for questions on the ramifications of these. It is a dialogue that continues to this day.

In the meantime, so characteristic of Greeks who turn away from the church but maintain some type of connection with God, I became a godmother to three children, two in the Greek Orthodox Church, one in the Unitarian Church. Somehow, somewhere, the words of Greek immigrant women I grew up with resounded in me throughout the years: "Remember, priests are not God, they are only men. Men make mistakes. Ultimately, God is what is important."

I have not resolved these issues. Each time I attend church services (which is perhaps once a year now on Holy Thursday—the last ten minutes of the service, because I enjoy the hymns and music that evening) my mind returns to the questions I had as a child, questions that, of course, have not been resolved, because they cannot be resolved outside an institutional structure. These questions are not simply my questions. They are the questions that many in my cohort and those cohorts and generations that follow and preceded, have. Unless the church opens a dialogue, these questions will remain unanswered for many who still struggle with their spirituality.

I must say however, that there are elements of the theology that sustain me. There is in many ways an affinity between the theology of Orthodox Christianity (at least the one I was taught in my pre-adolescence years and still read about it in more recent theologians) and elements of the Greek culture, the very elements I value. God as constitutive and constituted by a community of beings, the importance of community in the theology and the rituals associated with the church, the image of God as merciful and loving, as emanating from and giving life, God as the essence of life, God creating man (but what of woman?), who became part of God, the symbolic potential of this in each and every individual ultimately being sacred and thereby possessing an innate human integrity and value simply because he or she is human. These are the lessons I took from my grandmother's readings to me of her Bible. These are the basic principles I try to base my work on, whether in my research or in my classes.

In my writings on the church I am critical of the politics that parishioners engage in. Class and status politics on the local level often have negative effects on the well-being of the immigrant and working-class parishioners. Clergy and parishioners both try to further their material and other interests and so engage in politics of exclusion. To say that I have met sexist priests would be redundant, of course. I have also met racist priests, such as the priest who was relieved that "Greeks somehow now look lighter" than they did thirty and forty years ago. In a different research project I discovered that Wella and Loreal hair coloring as well as intermarriage by descendants of the earlier immigrant cohorts to northern Europeans have much to do with the Greek Americans' lightening and whitening process. It was also hinted to me that my work does not go down well with some of the converts to Greek Orthodoxy here in the United States.

At the same time, I must be fair and say that I have met many anti-racist priests, priests and laity concerned with issues of social justice. Our own Archbishop Iakovos walked alongside Martin Luther King in Selma, Alabama, in 1968. Social-justice-minded clergy and laity are, however, in these days among the more marginalized of the clergy and parishioners.

And yet, it is precisely as I delve deeper in my work, both research and teaching, that I find my need for "God" increasing. Sociological research takes a toll on the psyche. I find myself too frequently returning to the God of my grandmother. She daily reminded me, "God loves you, God is good." "Have faith in God and lighten your heart." "It is easier for a camel to go through the eye of a needle than for a rich man to go to heaven." The God of my grandmother, who told me about Magdalena, whom the villagers mocked and stoned but whom Jesus and God loved simply because she was human.

It is this God that I try to present to my son. It is the supplement to the religious and social instruction that my son receives in the afternoon Greek language and religion classes he takes at our local parish. It is an issue of focus, of emphasis. God, as the essence of life, constitutive of and constituted by a community of humanity. Next year my son will begin attending Sunday Catechism with his Greek afternoon class. Recently, he pointed to one of the little ceramic decorative pieces of the Three Wise Men. He asked, "Is this God?"

I said, "No."

He pointed to another and asked again, "Is this God?"

I responded, "No. These are the Three Wise Men who brought gifts to baby Jesus, just as people bring gifts to all babies because babies and children are special."

"Where is God? Who is God?" These are among of the many curve balls my five year old throws me on a daily basis.

I answer, "God is in our hearts, in our minds, God is all around us, God is in everything we see and touch. God is the essence of life."

He looked puzzled and asked, "God is in our hearts?"

"Yes," I answered. He looked satisfied for the moment.

My niece recently shared with me her newly acquired wisdom, "I have learned to separate the church from God. And you have to learn to, too."

On some level, I think that I do believe that my church can redeem itself in the eyes of women and of the marginalized in our society. It is there in the theology, it is there in the early history of Christianity and even during the Byzantine writings, as feminist historians of Greek Orthodoxy have pointed out. But it has not yet happened. And so, the phrase so often repeated during my adolescent years by Greek immigrant women still resounds in my ears: "Priests are only men. Priests are not God. What is ultimately important is God."

I still wonder how so many women who make this distinction, who taught me this distinction, can still bow down and kiss the priest's hand whenever a priest passes their way. While we make this distinction, the fact that our very history as a group is so closely intertwined with our church creates a situation in which we attend church, send our children to church services and catechism, but still remind our children, "Priests are only men. Priests are not God. What is ultimately important is God."

PART III

Opening the Ancient Treasure Box of Faith

8

A Life of Faith
and a Life of the Mind

MIRA MORGENSTERN

This chapter focuses on my attempt to integrate the various and seemingly contradictory aspects of my existence—the academic, the writer, the mother, the spouse, the community activist—as these influence and also express the challenges of living a dynamically religious, that is to say, G-d-centered life. Being a practicing woman of faith is challenging in every arena in which I conduct my life. In the avowedly secular world where I spend a great deal of my (professional) time, religious practice is viewed at best as a personal idiosyncrasy, at worst as a nuisance that hinders professional advancement and may even sabotage the full expression of clear thinking and intellectual attainment. In the religious community in which I continue to live and raise my family, participation in secular life—especially intellectual involvement in its pursuits—is viewed largely with suspicion and as potentially deleterious to maintaining perfect faith. As I have written elsewhere (Morgenstern 2000), I described the camouflage that I often don in order to negotiate the complicated terrain of my daily life, as a sort of "code" that enables me to "pass."

What are the moral implications of these negotiations? How do they facilitate the expression of a G-d-centered life? Many people of faith who work in the secular world opt to divide their lives into discrete parts, keeping their personal faith as far removed as possible from their professional concerns. In this sort of moral economy, professional attainment is held to possess no

---

Editor's note—According to the Halachah, defacing or desecrating the name of God in any way is forbidden. Thus, out of concern that a document containing God's name might not be treated respectfully, some Jews choose not to spell out the name in full. Indeed, some rabbis teach that this applies to the word *God* in any language. So some authors, as with Mira Morgenstern in this chapter, do not write the name of God (or Lord) where, for example, it might be thrown away. Instead, they use *G-d* or *L-rd*.

spiritual value of its own but is viewed instead as a (regrettable) concession to the necessity of economically providing for one's family. Concomitantly, the source of "real" spiritual worth is identified solely with religious practice, which is separated from the public manifestation of the workaday world. One obvious attraction of this approach is that it avoids oppositional encounters; upon returning home, one changes identity in much the same way as one slips into a different pair of shoes.

While this approach lends itself well to orderly flow charts of clearly demarcated life activities, I find that its actual substantive impact leads to a life of moral and spiritual schizophrenia. Circumscribing one's life into neatly demarcated boxes robs that life of the maximum attainment of spiritual vitality. My own life derives its force from the determination never to limit the extent of G-d's influence to any specific area; I believe that in order for life to retain its spiritual and moral coherence, G-d's influence must be acknowledged in every activity. Traditionally, the words of the Psalmist, "I set G-d before me always" (Ps 16:8), frame the Holy Ark at the front of the synagogue; in my opinion, these words must also accompany all quotidian activities, from the sublime to the banal.

As I see it, one's entire self must be involved with G-d at all times. Otherwise, one is in essence withholding full commitment to G-d. That attitude does not represent belief; rather, it exemplifies hedging one's bets. To my mind, this less-than-total commitment to G-d is precisely what is prohibited by the second commandment: "You shall have no other gods before Me" (Ex 20:3). This commandment means what it says: commitment to G-d must be unique and absolute.

The imperative of enacting G-d's pervasiveness in all life activities was brought home to me with particular force in a setting that at first glance seems inapposite: while taping a distance lecture to a college class in comparative religion taught by a colleague of mine in Arkansas. During the question-and-answer portion of the class, my colleague suddenly asked me to deliver a spontaneous English translation of the Shema, the central expression of religious belief recited several times daily by observant Jews. To recreate the scene, I include my translation of these ancient words (Dt 6:4–9):

> Hear, O Israel, the L-rd our G-d, the L-rd is One.
>
> And you shall love the L-rd your G-d with all your heart and with all your soul and with all your might. And these words that I command you today shall be on your heart. And you shall teach them to your children and speak about them; when you sit in your house and when you walk on the way; and when you lie down and when you get up. And you shall tie them as a sign upon your hand, and they will be phylacteries between your eyes. And you shall write them on the doorposts of your house, and on your gates.

In the course of complying with his request I found myself newly aware of the imperative to saturate each moment of the day with the presence of G-d.

The Shema prayer itself directs us to speak of G-d at all times with our children, "when [we] sit in [our] house and when [we] walk on the way; and when [we] lie down and when [we] get up." Traditionally, this is one of the first prayers taught to very young children, and I practice this by reciting the Shema even with my baby. "But he doesn't understand what you are saying," protested a family member when overhearing us. Not today, I agreed. But he already recites some words with me. As he grows these words will be part of his life, in his head and in his blood, suffusing his entire being. And then he will understand.

The practices of my faith involve more than just rote memorization or simplistic ritual fulfillment: they demand the dedication of the mind as well. At a time of unparalleled intellectual and technological achievement, it is ironic that much of the modern understanding of contemporary religious life appears bent on divorcing the intellect from service to G-d. This affects the more "moderate" accommodationist view of religion in contemporary life no less than the self-styled "traditional" approaches often characterized as fundamentalist or conservative. At bottom, however, both of these views— for different reasons—end up valorizing the separation of religious life from intellectual endeavor, which fosters just this sort of measured approach to G-d: the former, with its tendency to privilege the "rational" demands of career and modernity over the spiritual hold of religion; the latter, by emphasizing strict obedience to the hierarchy of religious leadership, at times to the exclusion of actual religious truth or individual soul-searching. In either case there remains no connection between the life of faith and the life of the mind.

Recently, however, I have had occasion to analyze one medieval interpretation of a particular biblical text that demonstrates the moral vacuity of the denigration of intellectuality in religious life. This biblical text is the well-known episode in Genesis when Jacob, escaping from the murderous wrath of his brother, Esau, dreams of a ladder on which angels ascend and descend, with G-d standing at the ladder's top promising always to protect Jacob and his descendants. At its most basic level, this dream has been read merely as wish-fulfillment on Jacob's part. However, throughout the centuries other interpretations have been proposed, many of them centering on the prophetic quality of Jacob's dream, its historical teleology, and the divine promise of eternal survival for Jacob's descendants, the Children of Israel.

In the twelfth century the great Jewish physician, Talmudist, and philosopher Maimonides proposed a novel approach to this text in his *Guide to the Perplexed*, interpreting it as a parable demonstrating that the participation of the intellect is crucial to the attainment of full spiritual development in the service of G-d. At first glance this reading of the biblical text appears counterintuitive; after all, Jacob is fleeing for his life, and is about to take up residence with a none-too-salubrious uncle of his in a foreign country. In that pressing context how can Maimonides claim that Jacob's dream centers on a rather esoteric notion of the role of the intellect in the service of G-d? In brief, the answer is that, for Maimonides, the movement of ascent described in the dream, reaching upward toward G-d, represents the movement of the soul toward its divine source. However, the soul's actual attainment of full union with its celestial origin is not guaranteed. According to Maimonides, success in apprehending the essence of G-d depends upon the extent to which one utilizes the power of the intellect—which for Maimonides is the closest measure by which we can express/apprehend the divine essence—to attain closeness with G-d. (In this, Maimonides alludes to the classical prophetic expression of attaining closeness with G-d: "understand[ing] and know[ing] Me" [Jer 9:23; also see Kimhi on this passage]). It is important to note that Maimonides does not confuse human expression of G-d's essence with the actual comprehension of that essence. That is why, according to him, the Bible uses the parabolic form to express truths that are too esoteric for human grasp.

A more contemporary expression of the role of parable in enabling the attainment of spiritual heights even in the quotidian aspects of our lives is presented by Rabbi Yitzhak Hutner in his collected lectures entitled *Pahad Yitzhak*. There, he points out that the parable is an important tool for grasping the spiritual meaning of what is seemingly insignificant and banal. I term this moral strategy one of "living parabolically." This enables us to avoid the spiritual desolation of artificially dividing our lives into (banal/secular) means and (spiritual/religious) ends. The ability to discern the spiritual truths behind seemingly pedestrian detail enables us to unlock the quiescent moral richness in these heretofore overlooked moments. The expanded self that results from this integration of means and ends leads to the spiritualization of all parts of our lives. In the end, an expanded sense of self allows us more richly to serve G-d.

This is the sense in which I view the totality of my academic enterprise as suffused with the service of G-d. It is easy for people to understand the preoccupation with G-d in my professional life when considering the public lectures that I give regularly on topics of biblical interest, some of which have subsequently been published in scholarly journals/collections. But it is more difficult even for sympathetic people, both within and without the academic and religious communities with which my life intersects, to comprehend that I view my "other" academic output—centering on the political thought of the Enlightenment—as an equally valid and valuable expression of divine service. I persist in seeing all of my work, the writing and the lecturing that I do, as well as my activities as a parent, spouse, and community member, as inextricable components of a G-d-centered life. As I view it, the fact that G-d grants specific talents to each individual carries with it a moral imperative—and not just a discretionary choice—to utilize that benefaction to its fullest extent. Thus, I see my academic work as being, in and of itself, an act of G-dly worship. In addition, the themes that I deal with in my work in political theory—the more nuanced view of the self that Rousseau developed in the eighteenth century and that proved so central to the modern understanding of the self; the interconnection between the personal and the political; the ambiguity that characterizes much of our modern understanding of the world and of the text—contribute to my understanding of the multifaceted messages that the Bible continues to hold for us in our own day.

Similarly, the harnessing of my personal life, anchored in family and community, to the service of G-d involves dedicating all aspects of my energy and mind to this goal. For me, the essence of raising children and of transmitting my faith to them is rooted in our continued learning of and appreciation for the ancient biblical and Halakhic texts on which our religious faith and practice is based. I want to inculcate in our children that practicing Judaism is not just preserving a set of old customs. More fundamentally, it encompasses a personal relationship with G-d that is expressed in the involved study of text, the performance of commandments and ritual, and active participation in community life.

As part of a married couple, I strive to uplift a relationship that can so easily become mired in the minutiae of car pooling and medical checkups, into a partnership that is spiritually nurturing, not just to the children that it engenders, but also to the original dyad at its nucleus. The community work that I do—involvement in study groups, prayer hotlines, and the provision of meals to families both in good times (the birth of children) and bad (personal tragedy)—is similarly impelled by the imperative to "walk in G-d's ways" (Dt 28:9). Traditionally, Talmudic sources (TB Shabbat 133b; TJ Sotah 14a) have explained this as the requirement of *imitatio Dei:* to imitate G-d in the performance of lovingkindness.

It is common practice to view the "personal" aspects of one's life—raising children, participating in a couple-based union—as anchored in pure emotion. I find, however, that the same intellectual force that impels me to include G-d in every aspect of my life similarly drives the love that I feel for my children. As I see it, the awe that one feels at the prospect of shaping another soul is an integral part of the love and devotion manifested toward one's children. And that requires a concerted intellectual effort, not the production of just vague spiritualized emotions. Maimonides expresses this most eloquently when he writes in *Guide to the Perplexed*, referring to the love for G-d, that love exists in measure to your grasp of it *("ha'ahava k'fi 'erekh ha'hasaga"* [III, 51]). In other words, if you truly love something or someone, then you are involved with that thing or person intellectually.

Recent philosophical writing has borne out this connection—as opposed to the classically held opposition—between the emotional and the rational: or, as one may prefer to express it, between the sentient life and the thinking life. In *Love's Knowledge* Martha Nussbaum points out that emotions are structured by cognitive elements and thus, strictly speaking, the two cannot be said to be completely oppositional to each other. In "Form and Content, Philosophy and Literature" (40–41) Nussbaum points out that this approach to the emotions can be read as Aristotle's understanding of practical reason. In an essay on love in the same book Nussbaum further suggests that emotion itself can embody a specific (material/experiential) type of knowledge

(268), as well as serve as the pathway to a new type of knowledge that is the foundation of community (272, 280–83). The link between the mind and the emotions is further explored by Eve Kittay in *Love's Labor*. In that book Kittay remarks that the humanity of her (profoundly retarded) daughter manifests itself in her capacity for love and happiness (152). It is no accident, I think, that these works questioning the traditional divide between logic and emotion, the mind and the body, are written by women in philosophy, people whose places in the discipline are traditionally marginalized and whose liminality is justified by the very nature of their (betraying) bodies (after all, according to the conventional wisdom, this is why no women were ever numbered among the great philosophers!).

I propose to take this logic one step further and recast the traditionally viewed oppositions, not just of mind and emotion, but also of mind and faith, as mutually supportive points along a larger continuum of human (self-) consciousness and existence. Interestingly enough, Kittay in her essay hints (perhaps unawares) at this connection when she writes of her daughter Sesha's humanity being manifest in her capacity for joy and love. Although Kittay does not utilize any specifically religious terminology, I think that she is talking about the presence of her daughter's soul, which I understand here as the defining essence of self and humanity. Importantly, humanity is here conceived as a state of being, rather than (just) a particular type of activity. Taking Kittay's disjunction between humanity and high-functioning intellect one step further, one may argue that the very presence of the soul indicates the existence of the human mind, broadly (and spiritually) understood. It follows that the expression of intellect (both narrowly and broadly conceived) is similarly an integral fulfillment of the human soul. In other words, mind and soul are implicated in each other, regardless of the extent of their functional capabilities.

Identifying the essence of humanity with the soul has complicating and paradoxical consequences. This understanding of the constitutive element of humanity means that humanity is defined not wholly in terms of its own self but also in relation to something greater and also outside of itself. For me, the source of this larger reality is the Divine. In my understanding, defining humanity completely in terms of its own needs and desires essentially belittles the individual, because it limits the individual to no more than another life-form, important only in terms of its own wishes. By contrast, defining the human by a reality greater than itself has several important consequences for the individual. It means that the human being can order his or her moral existence by a set of values that is not merely self-referential but absolute. This comprehension of human uniqueness has two corollaries, with widely differing political implications. Understanding the essence of humanity as deriving from the Divine allows us to accommodate other people by generalizing from our own apprehension of the radical alterity of the Divine to other human beings in the world. In other words, recognizing the Divine enables us to deal positively with other individuals in our own lives, since both G-d and other people are, to differing qualities and degrees, manifestations of

Otherness. Emmanuel Levinas has expressed it this way: "The absolute other is the Other. . . . God rises to his supreme and ultimate presence as the correlative of justice rendered unto men" (Levinas 1961, 39; see also 78). This approach yields a positive notion of community and a dynamically interactive political system. On the other hand, the radical alterity of the Divine has also historically facilitated the maximization of power in the hands of those individuals claiming to know precisely the exact nature of divine demands. As a result, G-d becomes the excuse for manipulation and exploitation.

But current conventional thinking refuses, for the most part, to acknowledge the mind-soul connection. In the contemporary Western world in which we live, the very introduction of religious concepts into an intellectually oriented discussion presents a problem. One facet of this discomfort is based on the widely accepted Enlightenment (Voltairean) view of religion as anchored in superstition and thus hindering its adherents from experiencing a more developed sense of their own possibilities. According to this critique, strict adherence to religion is essentially—or at least potentially—dehumanizing. Another aspect of the very real unease exhibited at the presence of religious ideas in public discourse is the result of the terror attacks of 9/11, where at least some of the sources of the terror were seen to grow out of a radicalized religious world view.

An increasing number of contemporary analyses of those modern-day examples of terror that proclaim themselves to be based on a particular—and to their minds, uniquely true—view of the demands of religion have concluded that this terror is actually a political statement disguised in religious trappings.* We may add, moreover, that the view claiming that it is morally acceptable and even right for some people to die in the fulfillment of the political/religious needs/views of others is, in and of itself, oxymoronic. From our Western, post-Enlightenment perspective, we recognize that this approach is a violation of Kant's stipulation that human beings be considered perpetually as ends-in-themselves and never as means to some other end.

The idea that human beings may function merely as instruments to realize somebody else's concept of political or spiritual perfection recalls the reactionary power structure characteristic of the divine right of kings. However, terrorism, even when expressed as a function of religion, embodies not the realization of G-d, but rather the negation of the Divine. Instead of respecting the other person, terrorism utilizes its power to abnegate the humanity of others. To the extent that the essence of humanity is reflected in its mirroring of the Divine, terrorism also marginalizes and denigrates the presence of the

---

* This is the assumption of Bernard Lewis's discussion of the "blame game" (see *What Went Wrong?* [New York: Oxford, 2002], 158–60, 1–7). See also idem, *The Political Language of Islam* (Chicago: Univ. of Chicago Press, 1988), esp. 82–90; Walter Lacquer, *The New Terrorism* (New York: Oxford, 1999), esp. 127–30, 142–44, 154–55; and idem, "Reflections on Terrorism," in *The Terrorism Reader* (New York: New American Library/Penguin, 1987), esp. 384–85).

soul in other people or, more concretely, in the Other. In other words, it is not just certain people who are considered sub-human and hence unworthy of life. More generally, it is any deviation from what is arbitrarily and unilaterally considered to be the only path to truth and justice that is condemned as evil and hence destroyed. The ultimate nihilism of the terrorist is to deny the moral autonomy of the divinely placed human soul.

It is especially important at a time like this to reintroduce the importance of religious concerns to public discourse, not in order to control such discourse, but in order to deepen it. I am speaking here of more than just the inclusion of undemanding generalities like *self-fulfillment* and *spirituality*, which can superficially substitute for a more complex notion of religious and spiritual life. Rather, I am referring to a dynamic notion of spirituality, including intense and deep-seated respect for all human beings, that emerges from à vital notion of G-d as the Creator of all being and consequently of all moral standards. I was reminded of this recently when reading an article by Harriet McBryde Johnson describing a series of colloquia on legalized assisted suicide and disability-based killing in which she participated with Professor Peter Singer at Princeton University. An avowed atheist, Johnson states that disability neither jeopardizes personhood nor predicts that person's quality of life (this is in answer to Singer's argument for allowing disability-based killing of infants). Interestingly enough, both Singer and Johnson valorize the idea of autonomy: Singer, for the parents of the putatively mortally disabled infant; Johnson, for the disabled person himself or herself. What, then, of the autonomy of the disabled person/infant who will never/again (re)gain consciousness? To this, Johnson replies that even in such an instance care can be a "profoundly beautiful" act for the caretaker (Johnson 2003, 55). In this connection, Johnson insists that the caretaker's economic and social position be constructed with care, a position not unlike that of Kittay in *Love's Labor* (chaps. 5–6). One may wonder what makes this act of caretaking "profoundly beautiful" in Johnson's terms, even when there is no (longer any) hope of autonomy on the part of the disabled. In the end I think that it is more logical to base Johnson's conclusion on the idea that respect for human life exists because that life is created by a divine Being and consequently bears a divine soul. With this approach human existence is safeguarded, since the inclusion of the Divine prevents human life from being limited to merely its own self-referentiality. Paradoxically—at least for us— the deepest expression of humanity exists when one permits G-d to enter the picture.

Most people in the Western world still are uncomfortable with the admission of G-d into the public domain, either because the history of arbitrary religious pronouncements by political powers gives them pause, or because religion's seeming irrationality scares them, and/or, perhaps most frightening of all, because the idea of morally reordering their lives to accommodate the presence of G-d appears profoundly unsettling. In this context it is worth remembering that the biblical text itself is replete with just this theme, particularly when the nascent Israelite nation is repeatedly warned, at the time of its settlement of the ancient Land of Israel, not to forget G-d or his commandments. This is more than just a series of threats regarding the resultant failure if these warnings should remain unheeded. Rather, the stories of the developing Israelite nation-state, particularly in the biblical book of Judges, reveal that to the extent that the Israelites ignore G-d in their attempt to establish a dynamic national life, they also prove incapable of relating to each other. For the Bible, G-d is an indispensable partner (even if at times a silent one) in forging and maintaining national discourse.

This line of thinking may ring strangely in modern ears. Perhaps this is because in modern times G-d is perceived as a divisive element in the overarching structure of the political nation. Religion is often viewed as tearing a nation apart: witness the German states in the seventeenth century; Canada in the nineteenth and twentieth centuries; Sarajevo and the Middle East in our own day. The *biblical* framing of this question, however, reveals another optic on this dilemma. It is worth remembering that in the Bible, ruling dynasties are not brought down for failing to obey one or another, or even several, religious proscriptions. For example, the kingdoms of David and Solomon are marked by various transgressions, and yet their monarchs remain beloved by G-d, because each of them persists in including G-d as part of the public discourse. As the Bible expresses it, it is the inclusion, not the exclusion, of G-d in the conduct of national discourse that enables the political enterprise to expand to include all of the inhabitants within its borders. Otherwise, it is all too easy to find a perfectly rational and even "humane" reason to withhold the epithet of personhood and thus of survival from any weak or disrespected group.

It might seem obvious to some to dismiss the textual analysis in which I engage as irrelevant in a world poised on the brink of all-out terror. Raising children in such a world seems more foolhardy than faith-based. As an observant and practicing Jew, I can never be oblivious to the real hatred facing me across the board from adherents of other faiths; domestic and foreign publications point this out to me every day. Even in my everyday existence, many people continue to react viciously once they discover that my lifestyle breaks whatever unspoken taboo tops their particular list: either of daring to engage in intellectual pursuits while endeavoring to practice a life of faith and of family-based connection; or of striving dynamically to engage in family building and faith practices while still maintaining an active professional life. The epithets thrown at these attempts to strive for an integrated personal/professional/spiritual life (in whatever order these may be assayed) eerily echo Foucault's affiliation of the "No" of the Father/ *"le non du père"* with the Name of the Father/ *"le nom du père"* (see Foucault 1962). The view that all of these areas—the personal, the spiritual, and the professional—are implicated in one another and that their achievement is mutually enhancing seems to threaten the dualistically divided either/or paradigm vigorously championed by those in positions of power. Perhaps this is because, in

Foucault's terms, this new approach to what is possible to accomplish in one's life disputes the secular/religious, professional/personal divide so identified with modern life; it challenges the order of permitted and forbidden actions *(le non du père)* stipulated by the males who are named as the source of authority *(le nom du père)*. Over time, this has led to acrimonious battles centering on my professional and/or social survival, which potentially can lead to alienating feelings of isolation.

Fortunately, I have been spared the depths of this despair. After years of dealing with these dispiriting encounters, it has occurred to me that for these people, no matter where they place themselves on the religious scale, the faith-based issues that form the core of religious concerns, like the social and political questions raised by the presence of women, are frightening when not kept securely in "their place," which is to say, the private sphere. It seems to me that people like this are essentially incapable of dealing dynamically with the Other—whether embodied by women, or alternatively, by the radical alterity of the Divine. For individuals of this persuasion, difference is frightening and must be controlled by them (or by their designated representatives) if their world is not to degenerate into chaos, which is to say, not conformable to their own ideas of what is proper. Therefore, they relegate these "disordering" factors—women, religious belief—to the private sphere, where the resultant powerlessness of women/faith issues is guaranteed by their categorization as subjective and hence irrelevant. In this view, *privatization* becomes a code word for control; women and religious issues alike are retained where they might be seen, that is to say, as maintaining the legitimacy of the patriarchal system in which they are forced to participate, but certainly not heard.

Proponents of this view fail to perceive that the "unimportant" and "ordinary" private-sphere activities—as exemplified by issues dealing with women and religious life—are themselves crucial for the ongoing and dynamic development of human creativity in all spheres of life, including and especially the public arena. As a result, the world as these powers "rationally" organize it is bereft of both personal responsibility and moral coherence. This sort of situation is highlighted in the biblical book of Ruth, which portrays the social fabric of the Israelite nation in a state of tatters: members of the Israelite community are distanced from each other, reflecting their leadership's alienation from their own people (Midrash Ruth Rabbah, Petihta 5). By contrast, Ruth's exemplification of the "ordinary" practice of *hesed*, or lovingkindness, is precisely what makes her extraordinary among the protagonists of that text. Ruth's valorization of ordinary decency, and her ability to extend lovingkindness to all other people, regardless of their provenance, marks her as the worthy progenitor of the Davidic dynasty. Lest this last point be read as relegating Ruth to the traditional "role model" for women, it is important to emphasize that the Davidic dynasty is viewed biblically as the ideal exemplification of monarchy. Hence, Ruth's position—as a stranger and as the founder of this dynasty—valorizes her role as the enabler of the renewal of Israelite community (see Morgenstern 1999). Ruth's ability to engage in other-directed giving while at the same time maintaining a solid sense of personal worth and moral autonomy makes her the ideal founder of a polity whose members are characterized by G-d as "strangers" (Lv 25:23). This expression, seemingly awkward for the illustration of community, which is defined primarily by whom it includes, becomes comprehensible when we recall that it is the acceptance of the Other—that is to say, what is generally perceived as *outside* the normal boundaries of inclusion— that most potently defends and guarantees our own humanity. Ruth demonstrates that the ultimate moral test of any community or polity is its ability to respect and include the Other. Ruth's ability to focus on self and Other, both in the service of G-d, allows her to found the dynasty that contains within itself the potential to transcend the limitations of history (traditionally, the Davidic dynasty is the source of the Messianic era).

In spite of its pervasiveness in the Western world of work and politics, the equation of women-connected and faith-based issues as manifestations of the Other, threatening the control of the contemporary holders of power, does not reflect the only challenge faced by professionally qualified women of faith. Often, opponents of women's quest for fulfillment in both their professional and spiritual endeavors simply refuse, categorically, to allow the full realization of even one of these enterprises. Thus, the glass ceiling emerges: women are promoted just so far but no further; women may "participate" in religious life, as long as they don't "aspire" to the status of clergy. To an extent, as Mary Douglas has pointed out, one may view the closed position of hierarchical institutions as logical outcomes of their structures (Douglas 1992). On the other hand, one may endeavor to recast the question so that, as Ruth has shown us, the fact that women actualize their own moral autonomy is perceived not as a social threat to the powers-that-be but as mutually fulfilling for all partners in the social enterprise. People who still fear women, and who therefore use their positions of power to restrain or destroy them, still do not "get" this connection. The pity is that, in the end, they deprive themselves of their own humanity. The tragedy is that in so doing, they erase the Other, as it is manifest in women, and by extension, the full experience of the Divine.

For us, these questions remain: Is it possible for our modern world, focused on the primacy and power of the self to the exclusion of the Other, to be redeemed? Does hope still exist for its people? Is there a role here for what Judaism calls *Tikkun Olam*—the repair of (what is broken in) the world? For me, the answer to these questions is finally yes. In dealing with all of these conflicts, I strive to remember that faith is not a palliative; rather, it is a constant and dynamic challenge. The biblical text of Jacob's dream reminds us that the imagery of the dream is of constant upward *and* downward motion. Similarly, along with the enervating interactions described above, I have also received much support from many friends and colleagues, whom I have met in both the personal and professional arenas.

One such instance comes regularly to mind: in bemoaning to my professor my attempt intellectually to master both "religious" and "secular" forms of knowledge, I cited the old proverb, "In the kingdom of the blind, the one-eyed are kings."

To this my mentor quickly replied: "You are not blind; neither are you one-eyed. You have one eye trained on each of the two worlds."

As I have come to perceive that the "two worlds" are merely different aspects of one complex unity, the difficulty of my self-appointed task has grown increasingly more apparent. Here, again, I find the biblical text of Jacob's dream most apt. As we review the narrative, we are clued in to the fact that while Jacob dreams of the heights of spirituality—the celestial angels climbing upward—his actual physical location is down on the cold, unforgiving earth, mired in his own troubles. Jacob's spirit soars upward; his body, however, remains encircled by rock. Jacob's condition reminds us of the perennial challenges that a life of faith encounters every day. A fundamental aspect of this challenge is to recognize the necessity to persist in our spiritual endeavors, even and precisely when we are forcibly occupied with issues of brute survival. In all of this we must take heed that while G-d promises to be with Jacob/us, it is still our responsibility to activate this partnership.

9

We Have the Faith
to Make Life Our Own

VICTORIA LEE ERICKSON

Now faith is being sure of what we hope for and certain of what we do not see. This is what the ancients were commended for. . . . All these people were still living by faith when they died. They did not receive the things promised; they only saw them and welcomed them from a distance. And they admitted that they were aliens and strangers on earth. . . . By faith the walls of Jericho fell, after the people had marched around them for seven days. . . . And what more shall I say? I do not have time to tell about Gideon, Barak, Samson, Jephthah, David, Samuel and the prophets, who . . . shut the mouths of lions, quenched the fury of the flames, and escaped the edge of the sword; whose weakness was turned to strength. . . . Women received back their dead, raised to life again. . . . Some faced jeers and flogging, while still others were chained and put in prison. They were stoned; they were sawed in two; they were put to death by the sword. They went about in sheepskins and goatskins, destitute, persecuted and mistreated—the world was not worthy of them. . . . These were all commended for their faith, yet none of them received what had been promised. God had planned something better for us so that only together with us would they be made perfect.

Therefore, since we are surrounded by such a great cloud of witnesses, let us throw off everything that hinders and the sin that so easily entangles, and let us run with perseverance the race marked out for us, our eyes fixed on Jesus, on whom our faith depends from start to finish.

—HEBREWS 11:1—12:2 (NIV)

Six thousand years is a long time. It is hard to imagine the world without Judaism, a way of knowing that has been examined, perfected continually, and passed down generation after generation. Acting on what we believe to be of *ultimate concern* shapes our lives and creates society as we know it. It is through faith and its practices that we come to make life our own. Christians, given the understanding of themselves as both born and adopted children of Israel, consider themselves to be inheritors of the stories of Moses, Miriam, Samson, Abraham, and Sarah. The Christian two-thousand-year-old messianic knowing of Jesus, Mary, Peter, and Martha has found a home in close to one third of the world's hearts. Islam also has its roots in Hebraic life and is now enjoying its own long legacy. Judaism, Christianity, and Islam have served the world as centers of codified and archived knowledge. The faith world produced mathematicians, astronomers, philosophers, theologians, chemists, lawyers, medical doctors, and many more specialists who often saw their production of knowledge as belonging to a divine knowledge base from which it was possible to understand the whole universe.

Inasmuch as we write out of our contexts and particularities, I am resisting the trend in the academy to narrow the context and the particularity from which scholars have the authority to write and to speak. I am convinced that the growing tendency to limit the authority of speech to a micro-specialization and to an even smaller world view (say to a North American, white, female, Christian one) is one developed out of fear of the Other, satisfied by controlling disciplinary boundaries around established knowledge bases. As the world speeds up the globalization of a shared knowledge, this is a disturbing trend. The Abrahamic religions have always sought to gather knowledge from across the world. The prophet Muhammad instructed scholars to go to China if necessary to get new knowledge, and he declared that the ink of scholars was as precious to Allah as the blood of martyrs. It is the ancient wisdom of the Abrahamic family that tells me that nothing can be gained when its most highly educated people are silent against the claims of a global need for knowledge, justice, and shared well-being. Learning how to speak in the face of degradation and oppression is our collective story as a people called out of slavery and into freedom.

The Abrahamic family created centers of learning in order to pool knowledge and provide self-critique. From these schools developed our current professional associations, wherein scholars give papers and work to understand one another's insight. The free voice of the academy is a hard-won right to democratic speech that is protected only by around-the-clock, global vigilance. When we prevent others from speaking, or when we choose to be silent, we betray the well-being of the whole community, which counts on its educated members to identify the return of danger as well as the appearance of the unprecedented.

A good example of religion's defense of the public right to speak and act is the history of the antislavery movement in the United States. According to Michael Young, rooted in and extending

> from the orthodox institutions of benevolence was a schema of the special sins of a nation. As they [the rights to speak and to act justly]

combined in the consciences of many evangelicals, they triggered confessional protests aimed at transforming individuals and national institutions. Evangelicals of an emerging middle class, and particularly women among them, were instrumental in combining these cultural schemas and triggering confessional protests. . . . Called out of this sphere of intimacy by conscience to exercise their moral leadership against forces that were threatening home and nation, the initiative of women brought the intimate register and the national register together with intensive and extensive power. (Young 2002)

The power of women to call forth democracy and reform, from both self and nation in public confession, was and is often attacked as "dangerous, upstart or ill advised" by their detractors but was and still is called "courageous and productive leadership" by their supporters (see Spain 2001).

We are often silent because we think that our contributions will not make the big changes and address the macro issues. We think that it is "only us the living" who are responsible for achieving the world we seek. We often fail to see that the eternal vision of peace that has been set out as the goal for us is accomplished over time as the generations work together to secure the peace. We build on one another's actions and historic community-based hope. What we know today is not only important for tomorrow, it is important to the production of knowledge that happened yesterday.

So I write from a global context and from a globalizing theology of the Christian tradition that hears the message given by the Prince of Peace as belonging to the whole world. More specifically, Christianity knows no national boundaries. Christians have the right, the responsibility, and the authority to address one another's behavior and to make recommendations for a better life. In this place I stand next to Islam, another globalizing religion that sees its message as one intended for all humanity. Next to both of us stands another ancient religion, secularization, born in the Garden of Eden, that competes with love-based, God-centered world views; but it need not, because all of these world views could work together in love and good will for the greater good.

Together the Abrahamic family of Islam, Christianity, and Judaism make up 60 percent of the world's peoples. It would seem, then, that we are at least 60 percent responsible for the well-being of the world. There were wonderfully creative times when we all got along, challenged one other's thinking, and advanced one another's lives and the lives of the non-Abrahamic world as well. As I write, it is clear that the world's neighborhoods still need help. Christians are called across religious, class, and cultural boundaries to bring aid to a suffering world.

I believe that there is no better way to live than to be of service to a God who simply wants us to love our neighbors, act justly, and be merciful. Left to myself, I am not sure I would do these things. That is why I need God's help. Even though it has its source in religious knowledge, there was nothing in my secular academic education that insisted that I serve a world in need of my intellectual resources. I suspect that this is true for many others as well. People of faith are "other oriented"; the secular modalities often encourage "self-orientation."

Even so, a claim to belong to a religious tradition does not mean that the one is a faithful member; some people believe that they can't have faith and trust others to believe for them. Nevertheless, from the beginning of time the people of God have been called to be like God, to "be there" for one another. This human-divine partnership works fairly well unless humans decide that they are God or that they don't need the God who calls them into deeper and deeper humanity. When I want to help others, I have access to six thousand years of wisdom traditions that tell me how my people have thought about the world, how it works, and how to build peaceable community while maintaining my identity.

As a sociologist, then, I understand the nervousness of some Muslims who are facing the global problems and opportunities found in what is popularly referred to as modernization. Modernization in the West was terribly uncreative and depended on secularization for its moral energy. Sociology's founding figures, Georg Simmel, Max Weber, Karl Marx, and Emile Durkheim, all addressed the anomie produced by the disenchantment that attended Enlightenment secularization and Western industrialization, both of which reoriented value systems away from human needs to the needs of capital. Secularization could have chosen a center other than capital; it could have chosen *neighbor love*, and it still can.

As a Christian I know that my empathy with the Islamic world is rooted in my church upbringing, in which human needs were central to everything one did during the day, whether the tasks were pleasant or unpleasant. Religion was at the center of life, directing the moral and ethical reasoning that shaped our everyday practices. Religion directs us toward loving-kindness.

Inseparable from religion were the religious and ethnic cultures that colored and gave rhythm to our lives. We mourn the ethnic and ethno-religious cultures that have disappeared. Urbanization, industrialization, and secular education are named as reasons for the disappearance of Norwegian and the other Scandinavian languages, festivals, specialty foods, and the old liturgies. Yet, given all of this, it is the religious instruction of my youth that has not disappeared; its moral and ethical demands are still clearly present and operating long after the departures of material culture and the people of blessed memory. This is precisely the hope that I as a Christian wish to share with my Muslim siblings in this current moment of cultural and social turmoil. It is possible to face what Max Weber called "the fate of the times," to change one's culture and society for the sake of survival in a changing world, and to survive with one's values, beliefs, and faith intact. Unlike my very small Scandinavian American world, the gigantic size of the Islamic world holds safe the prediction that its smaller subcultures will survive into the future as well. It is entirely possible for the Islamic world to democratize, modernize, and remain faithful.

In fact, we in the Abrahamic family of Muslims, Christians, and Jews are obligated to remain faithful listeners to the call of God in our lives as the world changes around us and with us. We all have theologies of hope. It is precisely our faith that challenges us to make the world as good as it can be. In our traditions every human being is valuable as one created by God, so everyone's voice must be heard and every person's ideas valued. From the beginning of creation we are, then, regardless of ethnic identity, oriented toward the life of the mind and toward democracy. One may see religious identity as larger and more powerful than ethnic identity.

Interestingly enough, on the other hand, the Norwegian state still sponsors the church and protects the dominance of Lutheran ethno-religious heritage despite the fact that it is now home to Muslims, Hindus, and Buddhists—and has always been home to Catholics. Its citizens are now examining whether or not they can remain democratic under these circumstances; for now, no one is too worried, as the religious majority is actively protecting the rights of religious minorities. However, in a much larger and diverse country like the United States of America we remain democratic precisely because we have separated the official actions of church and state. Even though we have very different and workable systems, in both Norway and the United States citizens believe that religion produces good democracy and democracy produces better religion.

One reason I continue to believe is that I must. My belief system's wrestling with ideas of how life should be lived has helped to produce the good and free society that I enjoy and want to pass on to my children and grandchildren. I do not see myself at all indebted solely or primarily to the last three hundred years of European American university-based secularized knowing. I and my people have developed spiritual resources and an expanding knowledge base that has survived the test of time.

The reasons for my "still believing after all these years" are many and, following the leadership of the College of New Rochelle Ursuline Sisters, I have divided them into three groups: experience, learning, and identity. First, my experience of the Holy, of God, remains profoundly real. Through worship I continually encounter a loving Creator whose hands are stretched out for mine. I see myself on a journey to the very heart of God. Second, I remain in faith communities even as they seem to be in the worst shape ever because I sincerely love the people who raised me up and sent me out into the world to meet other faithful who live by similar moral and ethical standards to those that I seek to maintain. Accomplishing the Christian mission of "bringing life and peace to earth" is intellectually challenging. Third, my identity, *who I am*, is elementally linked to early religious experience and training that formed the very foundation of my self-understanding, which continues to expand and become more deeply faithful. In short, I still believe because I continue to love those people who first loved me.

Societies change. Modernization replaced rural hand-to-mouth life with the steadier life of industrialization; despite these many socio-political-cultural changes, the call of God in our hearts remained the same. The call of

God to me and my response is a timeless spiritual experience. This spiritual experience is not itself religion. Religion is a social institution that dips into the well of our spiritual lives for its energy. My religion provides a well-traveled pathway for my faith's response to God. My soul life is more expansive than the cultures and societies I help create.

The word *religion* comes from the Latin meaning "to bind together"; religion unites what is broken apart. The word *pontiff* has a Latin root meaning "to bridge" what is separated. The primary role of religion in society is to make and maintain connections among people; it does this by teaching us how to love one another. It is difficult to study love sociologically. It is even more difficult to suggest convincingly that religion plays a major role in producing love in society when we are in the middle of global problems brought about by the tragic absence of love and respect between people because of interreligious strife. Nevertheless, one of the reasons I still believe is that the most loving people I have met are those who *believe in life and seek to give life to others,* regardless of where they stand on the believing and belonging continuum.

What is love, and why does it need faith? The dictionary tells us that love is an "intense desire for the other." Love is a kind of attraction and attachment to the other marked out by an embrace of the other, who thrives under its enthusiasm, grace, and mercy. Love is characterized by its confidence in and trust of the other. To believe in someone is to experience truth in that person and to be confident that he or she is trustworthy. *Faith* does not require logic or empirical evidence for its loyalty or for its ability to make promises. Faith, however, is also both logical and empirical as it is an action system of beliefs based on trust that forms the basis of our convictions about the seen and unseen world, its inhabitants, and the Holy. Faith is an act of grace, a true gift, a product of love's enthusiastic embrace. Jesus sums up what is expected of us by telling us to "love one another as I have loved you" (Jn 13:34). Love for the other mirrors God's love for us. It is through love that we build bridges to one another and to God.

It is only through love that we come to have faith as we trust the loving others to make the world a place we all can live in. The faith community that loves us and trusts us to embrace and nurture its members is the community that holds our "membership" or our "belonging." Memberships bring with them rights and responsibilities. The faith community is one where one's spiritual life, one's soul life, who one is, is safe and protected, nurtured and expanded, challenged and matured. The work that the faith community does in producing a believing adherent may be done for the sake of eternity, but society is the direct beneficiary of the loving person's embrace of others. The *network of embrace* is itself a community responsive to the needs of its members and therefore to the needs of society. The Abrahamic religious communities continue to establish hospitals and ambulance corps, schools and universities, libraries, hostels, day-care centers, social welfare agencies, and charitable foundations. Responsiveness to human need characterizes people of faith. One might argue that one does not need to be a believer to do good things. This is true. However, unbelievers number only 14 percent of the total world population; 86 percent of the world, then, finds religiosity beneficial and I would argue *elemental* to life itself. Yet, I believe that 100 percent of humans are spiritual beings and that people who do not believe or belong contribute from their own spiritual gifts to the whole.

The church, synagogue, and mosque are the critical and historic centers of educational systems that strengthen and sustain whole communities, societies, and cultures. The Abrahamic family sent its educational programs across the world. In many places of the world they still provide the only access to basic education. However, the division of labor between science and theology in the West was so dramatic that today the two rarely engage each other productively. However, as students' minds are growing and expanding, integrating and creating new knowledge, it is appropriate for the academy to develop productive tools for the classroom examination of the values upon which students act.

CLASSROOM STORIES

I will never forget the semester that I taught a sociology of religion class with the most amazingly diverse suburban student body I had ever had. Some young women from a minority sect sat in the back of the classroom and jumped out into the hall whenever they were afraid that what they were hearing would "destroy their faith." Their behavior delighted the liberal secularists to no end. Also in the back of the room sat a disheveled young person wearing oversize clothing, a cap over mounds of hair, and sunglasses—when I called roll I discovered gender identity when he answered to his name. The major assignment in this class was an ethnographic field account of a religious tradition not one's own. An Orthodox student had to get permission from his rabbi to complete the assignment (he later transferred to an yeshiva). One night after the class had departed, the man in oversized clothing came up to my desk and announced that he was not going to do the assignment, that he was going to do something else. He argued that he would learn more if he could go to a mosque, even though he was a Muslim. When I protested, saying that the point of the assignment was to learn about another religious culture, he shot back, "But you here have never wanted to learn about me." Spilling out of him came story after story about anti-Muslim behavior on campus and in American culture. He was afraid to be known for who he was. Every summer he returned to his Middle Eastern village, of which he said, "They are peaceful and kind; I hate coming back here."

So, I agreed. He could visit a mosque. The next week he returned with this report. He had arrived late to the mosque. With all the bad American images of Muslims in his head, he was afraid to ring the doorbell. It was the electricity of his body that rang the bell, he insisted, as his hand rested over the bell never touching it. It was a sign that Allah wanted him there. But who would answer the door? He had images of "Kung Fu" Muslim men opening the door and flying out of it only to chop him into pieces. As he stood there, afraid of what would happen next, the door slowly opened and light shown out. He looked down at a smiling six-year-old boy. The boy greeted him, "Salaam." The student told the boy, "I am late." "I know," said the boy. "I will teach you how to pray."

As the student reported the whole story to the class, everyone, even the secularists, had tears in their eyes. The three women in the back of the room said they too had a story. They shocked their peers by telling the class that they had gone to a "unity church" in the city. They had moved from fearing my lectures to placing themselves in a completely opposite religious world that challenged absolutely everything they knew. They claimed that they were made brave in the class and wanted to experience more traditions.

The liberals had surprises too. They shocked themselves and the class by describing their flight from a paradise-like religious encounter that was, they said, "the most peaceful experience" they ever had had. When asked why they left the church, then, they responded that they "had never experienced peace like that" and that they "were afraid."

The next week my Muslim young man appeared early before class. He had on new clothing, he had cut his hair, and the hat and sunglasses were gone. He asked for advice. He wanted to improve his grade point average so that he could go to law school. He said that the class gave him a pride in himself that he had never experienced before. He had dreams and visions for what Muslims could offer America.

Students are more ready to examine their spiritual worlds than we think and more in need of the exercise than they know. They need faculty who are willing to engage them and to challenge their hearts and minds to grow together. This is another reason why I still believe: I am witness to amazing transformations in people when faith comes alive in them.

CLASSICAL STORIES

Personal life commitments and religiosity, or lack thereof, of sociologists and the impact of these on the development of sociology are of great interest to me. For example, it would be difficult if not next to impossible to claim that Karl Marx held a religious faith of any kind. However, that does not prevent me, the believer, from seeing God in the person and the work of Karl Marx. Marx's relentless search for truth and the well-being of the poor not only fits the prophetic mold, but it mirrors back some of God to me in the body of this self-declared nonbeliever. The fact that Martin Luther was a role model for Marx, who thought he was doing a better job of reforming the world, is instructive. The same is true for Durkheim, the agnostic French Jew; Weber, the secularized German Calvinist Protestant; and Simmel, the wavering and wandering German Christian whose parents had converted from Judaism—all of whom took up the cause of the poor and the suffering. All of these theorists had well-established prophetic world views, and they sought to protect the social world from harm through their establishment of sociology as a discipline. I have argued elsewhere that Durkheim and Weber sought to use religion's ability to create solidarity by emptying religion of its contents, keeping its form, and filling it back up with secularized content (Erickson 1993). All of the great theorists have known that we cannot get rid of religion itself, because society needs a generative place for moral formation that is not directed by theology. We call their product civil society, where the freedom of the individual is of utmost importance and anchored in a democratic life not directed by theodicy.

One might see Marx's, Weber's, and Durkheim's struggles with and against God and religious traditions as profoundly religious activity that sought to bind up the brokenness created by the Enlightenment and urban industrialization. Marx sees himself donning the robes of the Great Monk; Weber crosses himself, a departing knight, as he dies; and at the end of his life, Durkheim holds out hope for religion. What would have happened to the discipline of sociology and to society, I wonder, if these great thinkers had let themselves be as free as Georg Simmel, another founding sociologist, and had examined religion from the point of view of the adherent, the believer? What would have happened in the West if instead of destroying connections, society and its educational institutions had built bridges into religious knowledge and therefore into the power of religion? These questions are profoundly alive in the Islamic world today.

SIGNIFICANCE OF GEORG SIMMEL

One of the reasons I still believe after all these years is that I have seen how, through sociologists like Georg Simmel (1858–1918), a self-critical yet affirmative and participatory understanding of the religious world contributed to the founding advancement of the German and American sociological associations and departments of sociology. Given the overwhelming participation of people in things spiritual, Simmel sought to understand the real-life connections between beliefs and the social world that are created when we act on our beliefs and values. He concluded that society is more than indebted to faithfulness; society could not exist for any length of time without faithfulness, without its members acting on interests bigger than their self-interest. What religion is, says Simmel, is "an attitude or a perspective" capable of bridging the rifts between people and their ideas (see Simmel 1997, xii). Religion reconciles the divisions between people, seeking stable relationships that work to make life possible for others. Religion does this work through its language, which engages people in public discussions, documents the world under their construction, and helps adherents name why they want the world to be this way.

Religion, Simmel says, has a special job in society of responding to pain and suffering. What science ignores, he says, are the other worlds that its methods cannot readily document and that it often leaves uninvestigated.

Simmel argued that life is co-constructed with God through the adherents' understanding of face-to-face encounters and what is expected of them.

In the Abrahamic traditions, when I meet you, I am required to see God in your face. This divine meeting decreases a learned human tendency toward fear and defensiveness and creates alternative access points to natural emotions of love and acceptance that open the self up to the other. When the faithful see God in the face of the other, the human need to create outsiders declines, along with the violence done to the outsider, as the other is invited into the inner circle of embrace and sociality. Building social kinship across differences, notes Simmel, is the work of religion and its love-based connections. Religion creates the society it envisions.

When religion is not embracing of the other, whose face is the face of God, something has gone terribly wrong with it, and society needs to know that too. Bad religion will negatively affect the social world. If educational systems stop engaging religion, there is little they can do to intervene in it when things go awry. If we use Simmel's empathetic model and explore people's theologies and indigenous sociological sensibilities on an ongoing basis, regardless of whether or not religion is our specific area of study, we may be rewarded by a deeper understanding of why people do what they do as we locate the place to which they submit their answers for their behavior.

COMPASSION STORIES

Several years ago, with several other Christian friends, I visited Muslim and Christian dialogue projects in South Asia. Our journey to see the best models for peace and reconciliation took us from a city to rough country roads and then to a mountain path that we walked up. We were two days early for the Christian village that hosted us. We had misjudged the time it would take to get there. By the time we arrived, it was nightfall. We were hungry. We had caught our hosts unprepared for us. There was no cooked food in the village. We all huddled together and wondered at the miracle of meeting other Christians. The Christian village had been carved into the top of a mountain and had a view that was breathtaking. But now, it was night and it was raining and we felt so far away from the resources we needed to end our hunger. Then, something interesting happened. Our host started to pray. As we prayed and sang, our hunger subsided, and we forgot about it. We started telling stories, and we laughed a lot. The wind kept hitting against the nipa hut, but we felt safe inside.

Then, we heard a noise. Our host opened the door a crack, and a horse popped its wet and dripping head through the door! There was a rider we could not see well. They exchanged words. The horse and rider disappeared into the darkness. Our host turned around and brought us a bucket of the largest blue-shelled crabs we had ever seen. We had food to nourish our bodies. Our host explained that they were a gift from the leader of the Muslim village whose people saw us coming and knew that we would catch our Christian host unprepared. So they went to the water and fished. The leader risked his own life on the slippery mountain slopes to bring honor to his friend and food to his guests.

Over the next few days we got to know these two villages, one that lived up the mountain and one that lived down the mountain. With the help of visiting seminarians, they had decided to read the Bible and the Qur'an and then to live the peace these holy books wanted. They built shared water wells, and they built a shared school. They protected each other, delivered each other's babies, mended each other's broken bones, and exchanged the riches of both mountaintop and valley. They answered to each other for the well-being of both villages. Then we learned the deepest part of their secret. They prayed. They listened to each other pray. They listened to the prayers they could not share in one voice, and they respected that difference. At the same time, they closed the gap, shortened the distance between them, by eating together at a shared table.

I still believe after all these years because I have often experienced my faith as the only key I have to a relationship with my neighbor. The Christian scientist has an extra boundary-crossing motivation that derives from a moral sensibility summed up as "your problem is my problem, and your joys my joys." I am not a scholar of Islam by any stretch of the imagination. But I am a faithful Christian who understands our shared history as taking a drastic turn for the worse at the end of the Middle Ages. In the name of all Christians who have passed on to eternity, I mourn the loss of the product of their labors that formed effective Muslim-Christian friendships and relationships of solidarity. It is because we spoke once together in local and university contexts that I feel that I have an obligation to speak again, not only because I have something to say to Muslims, but because they have something to say to me. There are hundreds, maybe thousands, of small Muslim-Christian dialogue groups across the world in villages, towns, and cities. These local efforts are critically necessary for the future of peace. It is disturbing, then, that scholars have not made the kind of impact on the daily well-being shaped by the relationship between Muslims and Christians as we have for Jews and Christians.

This is another reason why I believe and belong, a scholar-practitioner of faith: I listen to Muslim calls for "rightly guided" leadership and I know what they are talking about (see Lodhi 1989; Barlas 2002). Religious power is a complex of truth, beliefs, and practices lodged in trusting community-based relationships that expect people to "act rightly." Education, holy books, clergy, and scholars are key elements of producing a faithful, rightly acting community. Disruptions in any of these areas produces chaos in religion, culture, and society. The critical educational goal for Christians in the twenty-first century is to produce a scientist who maintains the values of the faith tradition and its heritage that created non-doctrinal science. Dialogue between them will perfect both theology and science as they "act rightly" together.

Islamic countries have witnessed a drastic change in community life. Lodhi writes: "We need to know why, in recent centuries, we have tended to be limited to imitation at best. We lack originality, what is in us that keeps us the way we are today while others are moving forward with ever-increasing speed" (Lodhi 1989, 2). Lodhi recognizes that a key problem is that Muslim intellectual leadership is understood to be living in the United States. The other problem named is that the educated no longer see the content of their education as Islamic. Western education is not anchored in Qur'anic understandings of human nature, natural law, Islamic teaching, and Islamic values. Lodhi calls for the "Islamization" of knowledge. It is precisely here that I connect with the pain of Islamic culture in transition. Segments of the Christian world have fought hard to maintain Christian schools, colleges, and universities; however, there are few institutions of higher learning any more that would claim to have courses in Christian economics or Christian biology. The Christian world stepped back and offered its colleges and universities (which make up the majority of the world's educational institutions) to the world. In so doing, it made room for Muslims, Hindus, Buddhists, Jews, and many more to come and study. One-third of the world's international students are Muslim (Lodhi 1989, 27). Western universities owe credit to the many Muslims who teach and study there.

It seems to me that the Islamic world needs to have a conversation with other religious world views that have traveled a similar journey. The Islamic historical memory of its own greatness is correct. It is also correct that science leaped ahead because it developed methodologies that allowed the world's scholars to study together internationally. Christian scholars in research universities who care about the welfare of Muslims might consider partnering with qualified faculty to develop research agendas that link Muslim scholars to peers and resources. The conversation between Christian and Muslim values in the context of non-doctrinal research would be rewarding in and of itself. The Muslim educational centers are largely in third-world countries that need partnerships with the First World that do more than steal away their intellectual wealth.

So, why should Christians worry about the crisis of thought in Muslim countries? First, we are a religious family that transcends all boundaries. A diverse and often argumentative family, but a family nonetheless. When a family member feels humiliated and that something is missing from life, it is our duty to respond. Second, helping the Muslim academy regain the eminence it cherished in the past is to the world's benefit. Third, the courage and hard work it would take to achieve a revival of Muslim scholarship would develop positive virtues in Western scholars, starting with humility, patience, and commitment.

The lovely thing about being a Christian is that we are called, and we call ourselves, to be active in the world for its benefit. God's work through us to bring healing and reconciliation to a broken world is reward enough for the cost of discipleship. Applying our professional and academic knowledge to these tasks is an act of stewardship. Many Christian scholars are quietly doing just that all day, every day, in their search to understand and to affect, for example, at-risk youth behaviors, crime, spouse abuse, cult formation, labor law, drug abuse, pharmaceutical demands, solar energy needs, urban economic development, and much more.

That is the one gift I wish to give younger scholars—permission to use the passion and/or insights of religious knowledge in their theoretical, documentary, and applied work. I have worked for many years to understand the intersections of violence, religion, and crime. My personal, professional, and academic understandings of criminological formation and reclamation have combined in useful ways that merge a theoretical sociological understanding of the sacred text, faith, and belief systems with an applied clinical sociological approach to using these in a Sing Sing prison program (see Erickson 2002). When asked to reflect on the program, one inmate wrote, "I still have a useful life to live." That is what believing and belonging provide for me— a way to be there to help others make life their own.

10

"You (Don't) Gotta Have Faith"

Intergenerational Jewish Feminist Research

DINA PINSKY

Jewish second-wave feminists are an interesting group to study because while they were fighting for women's rights in the United States the Jewish community was lagging behind in its move toward gender parity. But not for long. The second-wave feminist movement had a major influence on American Judaism. Jewish feminists used mobilizing skills learned from feminism and other social movements to push successfully for change within the Jewish community. These changes took place at the level of standards of practice within the so-called liberal denominations—the Reform, Reconstructionist, and Conservative branches of Judaism.

Throughout Jewish history women have been prohibited from filling honored religious positions. Synagogues and study halls, the centers of Jewish communities, were male-only spaces. Jews pray three times a day, and a quorum of ten is required for the most holy prayers to be recited. Traditionally, women did not count in a prayer quorum. Moreover, they were not allowed to lead services, which is an honored position. Not only that, they were not even allowed to be in the synagogue unless they were behind a partition, out of sight of the men, lest the men become sexually aroused by them. They were also not allowed to serve as witnesses for Jewish legal matters.

Feminist theorists have observed a division in Western cultures between public and private spheres. The gender dynamics of many societies are divided along these lines, with women in the private sphere and men in the public sphere. This public-private split applies to Jewish religious law as well. Public Jewish life was designed for men. Girls and women were seen as outside the realm of public recognition and ritual life. For instance, important life-cycle rituals at birth and puberty, like the bris and bar-mitzvah, were designed for men, with no equivalents for women until the mid-twentieth century.

Women were thought to be passive observers of public Jewish life. Their place in Jewish observance was intended for the home. However, interestingly enough, when civil matters were governed by Jewish law, women were permitted roles in the public sphere, such as business and property ownership, that were prohibited to their non-Jewish neighbors (Hyman 1995). So, for instance, it was not taboo for Jewish women to operate in the public sphere by running businesses, like my immigrant great-grandmothers, who helped run their family stores. However, in the synagogue they were not permitted to lead services or be counted for a prayer quorum.

While the study of the Torah was seen as the highest pursuit for a Jewish male, it was considered unseemly for a Jewish woman. Women were not allowed to learn Jewish texts, beyond what was necessary for keeping a kosher home and socializing the children. The ironic result is that when Jews immigrated to America, Jewish women were often the breadwinners for the family while the men studied Torah all day. Being a Torah scholar is the highest status position a Jewish man can have within Judaism. But Jewish women with jobs at the beginning of the twentieth century in capitalist America were primed to influence the American feminist movement.

In the second half of the twentieth century Jewish feminists organized Jewish leadership and influenced massive transformations in modern synagogue life. The prohibition on gender equality in many synagogues has been abolished, so that women now enjoy roles in the synagogue that had been prohibited to them for thousands of years. Most synagogues outside of the Orthodox community are now gender egalitarian (Wertheimer 1996). Women now count in a prayer quorum, are permitted to lead services, and read Torah and generally act as equal participants in the synagogue. The vestiges of a male-dominated patriarchal Jewish culture do still remain, and in Orthodox synagogues women are still second-class citizens, but even in this most traditional branch of Judaism small steps are being taken toward allowing women increased opportunities.

Not only did the roles within the synagogue move toward gender equality, but the ultimate position of leadership, the rabbinate, opened up to women as a result of the second-wave feminist movement. In 1972 the Reform movement ordained its first woman rabbi and in 1974 the Reconstructionist movement followed suit (Fishman 1993). The Conservative movement did not ordain its first female rabbi until 1985, but this change was a result of the activism of feminists who began protesting in the 1970s. So, while women have long been prohibited from public Jewish life, we now serve in every capacity as leaders of Jewish communities.

These trends, women's occupation of Jewish leadership positions and ritual equality in the synagogue, are tangible improvements in the structure of Jewish institutions that have resulted from the Jewish-feminist movement. The Jewish-feminist movement has also provided the space for women's creative and spiritual innovation, including the development of new rituals and Jewish-feminist cultural production such as art, literature, theater, and music. The availability of Jewish education to women and the ordination of women have added the perspectives of women to Jewish religious culture.

Another transformation in American Judaism is the result of the impact of feminism on Jewish thought. Jewish-feminist scholarship has proliferated in many areas in the past twenty years, including such developments as feminist interpretations of Jewish texts, Jewish feminist theology, gender-inclusive liturgy, and the creation of feminist rituals.

For my dissertation research I interviewed Jews who had participated in the feminist movement of the 1960s and 1970s. In many ways, because of feminism, Judaism is not the same religion as it was in the 1930s through the 1950s, when the participants in my research were growing up. Most of these changes have taken place in the past thirty years, which results in generational differences among American Jewish women in terms of their exposure to egalitarian Judaism. While the generation of second-wave feminists saw the feminist transformation of Judaism in their lifetime, most of the feminists I interviewed were not directly involved in feminist activism within Judaism. By the 1960s many had become disconnected from the Jewish community as they became immersed in the activist community. Moreover, their past experiences with Judaism had taught them that it was full of traditions that were antithetical to the ideologies of the New Left. So many of the women I interviewed had written off Judaism as sexist long ago.

Research on Jewish identity, such as mine, can only be studied in the context of this social history. For feminists of any faith, belief gets mediated through experiences with patriarchal religions. Religious faith is developed in the context of the cultures in which the groups live. Research into "faith" of any sort should take into account the history of the religious group being studied and the social milieu in which it has operated.

INTERGENERATIONAL RESEARCH

Jewish identity is not particularly about faith or belief. In this book about feminists of faith my story of researching Jewish identity among second-wave feminists seems oddly out of place. You might wonder how I can study identification with a religious group without focusing on religious belief. The story gets complicated when it becomes about defining what it means to be Jewish—and to what extent this identity is related to or separate from religious belief.

Researching religious identity involves suspending definitions of religiosity and preconceived notions about how people relate to their faith. My research involved a group who identified as Jewish. However, many of my informants would not claim to have "faith" of any sort.

Most of the Jewish feminists I interviewed were born between 1930 and 1950. Not surprisingly, since the vast majority of Jews in the United States are descended from immigrants who came to these shores at the turn of the twentieth century, the people I interviewed are children and grandchildren of immigrants. Although I too am a Jewish feminist, I am a generation or more younger than my interviewees, born in the early 1970s, and thus my experiences as an American Jew and a feminist have been quite different from theirs.

When I read the novels of authors like Bernard Malamud, Philip Roth, Saul Bellow, and others who wrote about the European Jewish immigrant experience, I became fascinated by the influence of one's generation in America on Jewish identity. A common theme in those novels is the struggle, on the part of the children of Jewish immigrants, to assimilate and lose their parents' "greenhorn" ways. Yet I knew that American Jews of my generation, the grandchildren and great-grandchildren of immigrants, were romanticizing and embracing the very customs that their parents or grandparents tried so hard to distance themselves from. Among my generation there has been a movement of "return to Judaism" called the *baal teshuvah* movement, in which young Jews choose to be substantially more observant than their parents. The Orthodox movement has grown in numbers in the past twenty years because of this movement (Davidman 1991). Even among non-Orthodox young Jews, I have seen a trend among my peers toward becoming more actively Jewish than one's parents.

This generational push and pull between welcoming and rejecting Judaism and Jewish culture is of particular interest to me as a sociologist. The Jews of my generation who became Orthodox did not act in a vacuum. Instead, they were influenced by historical events, their social situations, and the actions of others in their communities. Likewise, the Jewish identities of the cohort that I studied followed a typical pattern in response to the social contexts of their generation. My interviewees were influenced by the immigrant generation's struggle to balance the old world and the new. As the first and second generation in the United States, many of them were pushed to assimilate into mainstream culture by downplaying their Jewish difference. To add more ambivalence to their idea of being Jewish in America, when they participated in the social protest movements of the 1960s and 1970s, they found that religion was considered passé and criticism of Israel was fashionable.

At the same time, a resurgence of identification with ethnicity and minority group status was taking place in this country. American views of cultural difference were changing from the melting-pot model of assimilation into the majority culture to the salad-bar model of valuing multiculturalism. So New Left Jews were confused about how to think about being Jewish. On the one hand, religion was out and Israel was considered a political enemy; on the other hand, being an ethnic minority was in.

From my oral history interviews I learned that many feminists went through the 1960s with very little awareness of themselves as Jews. They downplayed their Jewish identities to others and also to themselves during this period. When they spoke about this period of their lives, they commented that it was a phase in which they never went to synagogue or observed holidays and did not think very much about being Jewish. Yet later, as the multicultural movement began to inspire people to think about their cultural identities, many Jewish feminists followed the lead of African American, Latina, and lesbian feminists and started reflecting upon what it meant to be an "othered" feminist. This trend is evident in autobiographical writing by Jewish feminists of this cohort.

As a sociologist I am fascinated by social movements and collective identities. While Jewish identity is an individual's relationship to being Jewish, it is strongly shaped by factors external to the individual. The generational effects on Jewish identity that I have just described demonstrate how the identities of individuals are inextricably linked to their social cohort and world events. Whole generations of American Jews who experienced the same events reacted similarly in terms of their attitudes toward being Jewish.

THE VIEW FROM THE SO-CALLED THIRD WAVE

My experiences growing up Jewish are in stark contrast to the experiences of women of previous generations. Although I attended Jewish day school and a Conservative synagogue as a child, I was not even aware of gender inequality in Judaism until I was a teenager. While many of my research participants had no choice but to experience a Judaism in which they were second-class citizens, I was pushed to be an active participant in services in my synagogue and day school with no distinction from my male classmates.

In my Jewish day school, girls were required to learn the same material as boys and to participate fully in religious services. Since I had a strong voice and good Hebrew skills, I was often asked to read Torah and lead services for our elementary school daily service. This sometimes felt like a burden rather than an honor. There were times when I just wanted to sit with my friends and pass notes during services. I may have felt differently about leadership roles if I had been aware of the fact that what I considered chores— leading services, carrying the Torah, and reading the Torah—were actually honors that had been off-limits for other girls and women for all of Jewish history until my mother's generation.

Unlike the feminists I interviewed, by the time I arrived on the Jewish scene I was able to benefit from the feminist transformation of Judaism. Many of those I interviewed complained that their brothers were sent to Hebrew school and given bar-mitzvahs whereas they were not. However, I had the same opportunities for Jewish education and participation as my brothers. Moreover, after I was bat-mitzvahed, I taught other children in my synagogue to prepare them for their bar- and bat-mitzvahs.

I first came in contact with non-egalitarian Judaism when I was fifteen years old. My first shock was while leading services on a trip with my Jewish youth group when I was asked to step down and stop leading so that the "holier" parts of the service could be led by a boy. Then, in Israel as a sixteen year old, I was surprised to hear my friends tell me that the beautiful soprano voice we heard singing in the Great Synagogue in Jerusalem was actually a little boy because women were not allowed to lead services in Orthodox synagogues. I was raised to feel as comfortable in a synagogue as in someone's home, yet this was my first time at an Orthodox synagogue. And I was surprised to find myself naive to certain Jewish customs after years of Jewish education. Why had I not learned about gender inequality in my own religion? I am now grateful that I remained naive to the sexist traditions of Judaism until adolescence, because it gave me the opportunity to develop a love for Judaism and to feel valued as a Jewish girl.

My adolescent experiences in non-egalitarian Jewish settings caused feminism to begin to foment within me. I attended an Orthodox high school for eleventh and twelfth grades. There I found myself frequently fighting with the rabbis to teach me Talmud. However, I was unsuccessful; they refused to teach me Talmud because I was a girl, and they argued that it was unnecessary material for me to learn. If I wanted to learn something having to do with the dietary laws or other domestic issues that would pertain to me as a girl, then they would be happy to take on another topic of independent study with me, they explained. Although when I was a kid I had resented being asked to lead services, I quickly learned as an adolescent not to take participation in public Jewish life for granted. I came to realize that, for Jewish women, simple actions like wearing a prayer shawl, chanting from the Torah, studying Talmud, or even being counted in a prayer quorum can be feminist acts in and of themselves.

MEASURING JEWISH IDENTITY

Since Judaism favors observance over belief, the sociologist of Jewish identity is presented with a challenge in measuring emotional and affective dimensions of Jewish identity. There is quite a difference between observing belief and observing behavior. Jewish observance can be directly observed, unlike spiritual belief. As a graduate student working with studies of Jewish identity, I learned that most community federation surveys of Jewish life measured Jewish identity by identifying a list of practices. These surveys included the following items in an index of Jewish identity: Do you use separate dishes for meat and dairy? Do you refrain from handling money on the Sabbath? How often do you attend synagogue services? Questions of meaning and feelings about Jewishness were not part of the measurement of Jewish identity.

Measuring Jewish identity requires a unique conceptualization of belief, religious observance, and relationship to God. If I had given my informants the Jewish federation surveys, some would have had a difficult time answering the questions on practice because their practice varies from year to year. Moreover, the same informants who referred to themselves as either "not very Jewish" or "very Jewish" would seem identical to each other in terms of Jewish practice. The label "very Jewish" seems to refer to an intangible attitude of identity salience that would be difficult to observe in the research process. Belief, observance, and strength of identity are not necessarily correlated.

Ethnographers have written extensively on the role of similarity with and difference from informants in the research process. I was both insider and outsider with the group I studied. On the one hand, like them, I am a Jewish feminist. But a large part of the interview process focused on experiences in the women's liberation movement, which made the age difference between us obvious. For those who are more observant or more closely affiliated with synagogues, the interview brought out our similarities. We drew on a common Jewish lexicon. Nevertheless, interviewees of all types used Yiddish and Hebrew words with me, assuming that I would understand words and cultural references that many other Jewish researchers might not.

There was an unspoken comfort level because of the ethnic culture that we shared. I think that my similarity to the research sample provided a methodological advantage. Since I am both Jewish and feminist, I was able to speak the same cultural language as my informants and to understand the context and meaning of their narratives with ease. We drew on a shared ethnic heritage, which consists of not only religion, but also language, history, art, music, food, and so on. This provided a level of connection with religious and secular informants alike. Randi, one of my interview subjects, grew up in a very assimilated Midwestern Jewish family and had anxieties about not seeming "Jewish enough" in comparison to others. Her practice of Jewish customs was almost nonexistent, and she claimed to have a "dislike of religion." Nonetheless, Randi still considers herself Jewish: "Nothing would ever make me renounce Judaism because I am a member of that tribe that started back there that Moses led out of Egypt."

And there were other informants who explained that while they do observe some Jewish holidays or other religious customs, they do so as a cultural expression rather than as a religious observance. Being a secular Jew for them is largely a matter of personal interpretation; their purported motivation for Jewish practice is ethnic identity. For instance, Eleanor explained that she takes Rosh Hashanah and Yom Kippur off from work every year. However, she added the caveat, "And that's more a way of saying that I'm different from other people. It's a cultural diversity issue more than anything else." For Lisa, it is her social life that reflects her Jewish identity: "I'm not a religious Jew. I don't go to temple and my contact with Judaism is cultural. . . . Unfortunately, I think the most telling thing about me being a Jew is that I have very few friends who aren't Jewish. Very few."

Passover is one of the holidays observed by the most Jews (Kosmin 1991), and many of my secular informants mentioned a fondness for the liberationist messages of this holiday. Eleanor: "We've never been involved with any synagogues or anything. We've always celebrated Passover kind of as a Jewish Thanksgiving. And we've always made our own *hagaddah* [the text of the

Passover service or *seder*], which has been kind of, you know, progressive and changes year to year and things like that." Evelyn also expressed an affinity for celebrating Passover despite the secularism of her family: "I was very antireligious. . . . But we always had a *seder*."

I am like many Jews in that I think of myself more as an "observer" than a "believer," even though I do believe in God. What does this mean? Jews have a unique relationship to the concepts of belief and faith. A good Christian must believe in Jesus, but to be a good Jew, it is not required to believe in God. In fact, there is no essential doctrine dictating what Jews are supposed to believe (Gillman 1990, xx). In Jewish lingo a religious person is more likely to be called a "practicing Jew" or an "observant Jew" than a "person of faith." In fact, the word *faith* sounds oddly Christian to my ears. It is not a word used often by rabbis in sermons, by people talking about Jewish identity, or by many Jews to describe their own relationship to their religion. Jews may refer to being Jewish as their religion or ethnicity, but not as their faith. Nonetheless, the word *faith* is used by Americans as a synonym for religious affiliation of any type. It is common to refer to someone as being "of the Christian faith" or "the Jewish faith" or "the Muslim faith."

The difficulty I face in writing about faith and Jews is about much more than semantics. Belief is not the central measure of Jewish identity because Judaism is a nationality as well as a religion. Jews have been set apart as a minority group in every country they have lived in for thousands of years. This history of peoplehood has resulted in a sense of ethnic solidarity among today's American Jews. Being Jewish is a cultural identity that extends beyond the religious aspects. Many Jews identify as secular nonbelievers and non-observers of Judaism yet still feel strongly Jewish.

This feeling was common among my study participants, many of whom identify as secular Jews, using the term to imply that their affiliation with Jewishness is cultural rather than religious. American secular Jewish identity can be traced back to the Haskalah movement or the Jewish enlightenment. The Haskalah movement, beginning in the eighteenth century in Western Europe and the nineteenth century in Eastern Europe, emerged from the European Enlightenment. In European cities during the Enlightenment many of the restrictions against Jews were relaxed, and in some cases, they were granted citizenship and allowed into high schools and universities (Feiner 1996, 62–88). The Jewish members of the Haskalah movement advocated the acculturation of Jews into mainstream societies. For the first time in Jewish history, peoplehood and religion could be separated for Jews (Cohen and Eisen 2000, 31). The result was a group ideology that rejected the Jewish religion; emphasized a Jewish nationalist identity; and advocated Yiddish language, literature, theater, and culture. This ideology is the predecessor of secular Jewish culture in America today.

Members of Jewish secular movements emigrated from Europe and came to the United States at the turn of the century, and their movements continued to flourish here. These many secular and progressive Jewish groups included labor Bundists, Yiddishists, and secular Zionists. Those groups influenced the founding of contemporary organizations of secular Jews such as the Society for Humanistic Judaism and the Congress of Secular Jewish Organizations (Silver 1998). In this country there are still secular Jewish institutions that have been in existence for a century, including *shulas*, or afternoon schools teaching Yiddish language and secular Jewish culture, and socialist Jewish camps. They emphasize the transmission of Jewish culture through social justice, language, food, and cultural expressions such as folk music, dance, plays, and literature.

Although the focus of my research project was Jewish identity, I did not plan to ask whether my informants believe in God. I knew that religion was an uncomfortable subject for many in the cohort I studied and that religious belief is an extremely personal issue. Thus questions of faith were not explicitly part of my interviews. Although I did not include a question on whether one believes in God, distinctions of faith were pronounced by the feminists I interviewed. They clearly labeled themselves as certain types of Jews. In addition to referring to themselves as secular Jews, I also heard labels such as "cultural Jews," or "politically Jewish"; or one woman humorously called herself a "culinary Jew." To be a secular Jew is to identify with the Jewish people, culture, ethics, and history rather than with the spiritual aspects of the Jewish religion. To a Christian, *secular* implies atheist. However, even a few of the religious informants claimed to have atheist tendencies.

I am often surprised to hear people call themselves atheists just because they do not believe in a supreme being imagined as an old man with a long beard and a staff that emits bolts of lightning. This is a very simplistic definition of God. Many of these self-claimed atheists do, however, believe in the oneness of all being, or a spiritual force in the universe, or think that there must be "something" out there; nonetheless, they insist they are atheists. To me, this demonstrates the lack of discussion in our society about God. Secular Jews who are not affiliated with Jewish institutions or synagogues often possess simplified notions of Jewish spirituality absorbed from their childhood experiences with Judaism. Consequently, they, along with other Jews, feel that in order to believe in God, they must believe in the fire-and-brimstone God of the Hebrew Bible.

In actuality, for thousands of years Jewish tradition has incorporated many other views of God—from the kabbalistic view of the omnipresent God who is part of everything and in all of us *(ein sof)* to the concept of *ayin* or mystical nothingness (Matt 1996). Each generation has crafted a vision of God based on its culturally based understanding of the world. During times when there seemed to be no order to nature because of a lack of understanding of the workings of the physical world, God was a scary taskmaster and punisher. And during times when kings reined supreme, God was envisioned as a king.

Many of the feminists I interviewed came of age during and immediately after the Holocaust. Like many of the reports from Jews who survived the Holocaust, they found it impossible to reconcile the horror of that event with the possibility of God. Olivia, the daughter of immigrants from Eastern

Europe, was already questioning the existence of God when she read *The Diary of Anne Frank* as a young woman. Olivia said: "Then I really was reinforced in my ideas that if all this could happen, there cannot be a God. And certainly not a Jewish God. So that was reinforced and I was, I was estranged. I would not convert. I was very proud to be a Jew. I identified myself as a Jew, but I was an atheist. And I still am."

Rhonda is also the daughter of immigrants from Eastern Europe. She spoke of the tensions growing up as the only child of a secular communist father and an Orthodox mother. She attended a secular socialist/Yiddishist afternoon school. Rhonda followed her mother's Orthodoxy throughout her childhood and defended her belief in God to her father during feisty family debates. However, when Rhonda was a young woman, beginning in college, she started to question Judaism, eventually becoming a secular Jew. She now describes herself as "allergic to religion." Rhonda explained the roots of her atheism: "And I know that the fact of the Holocaust is what made me an atheist. Because if God is good, he's powerless. And if he's powerful, then he's no good. And that just did it for me. That really did it for me."

Jennifer also traced her atheism to the Holocaust. She told me the story of a defining moment in her life when she was about seven years old, watching "the uncut, unedited film of a liberation of the concentration camps" in Sunday school. "It traumatized me. And I decided then and there that if there was a God, I wasn't interested. The leader God could intervene in history and chose not to for whatever reasons, none of which were good enough for me. Or God couldn't intervene in history, in which case God wasn't God. But I lost whatever faith I had, religious faith I had, at that moment, on that day, in that auditorium, with those images in front of me."

These secular Jews who do not believe in God and only engage in minimal practice of Jewish customs are still Jews. Judaism does not write off nonbelievers. The Jewish religion stresses the tangible—observable practice over belief. The *mitzvot*, or commandments, which are the cornerstone of Judaism, dictate everyday actions from what one can eat to business ethics. However, thought and belief are considered to be under the control of the individual. Unlike Catholicism, which requires belief in core tenets in order for one to be considered Catholic, the sages of the Jewish tradition did not believe that belief could be mandated. Don't get me wrong—belief in God is central to Judaism, it is just not necessary to consider oneself a practicing, observant, or even religious Jew.

My agnostic or atheist informants appreciated this aspect of Judaism. As an example of this dichotomy between belief and practice, one informant reported that even his rabbi considers himself an atheist. When Mark asked his rabbi what he does when he prays, the rabbi replied, "I'm an atheist. I'm not praying to God. I'm praying to the wholeness of being."

Ironically, for a Jew questioning one's faith can be particularly Jewish. The rabbis of Jewish tradition welcomed active debate with the religion. In fact, the rabbinic commentators on the Torah and Mishnah maintained the custom of *makhloket*, or arguing within the text. In the rabbinic tradition, the basis for contemporary Judaism, there are varying interpretations for each law and multiple readings of each issue. The Jewish tradition values questioning, even of itself, and the minority opinion is often maintained within Jewish legal texts. Each generation is given the opportunity to bring social factors into consideration in deciding religious issues.

This tradition of dissension has given rise to the acceptance of the contemporary Jewish-feminist movement within institutional Judaism. Paradoxically, while the tradition emphasizes continuity with the past, it also makes room for innovation and has repeatedly done so throughout history, sometimes quite radically (see Hauptman 1998). Though the Jewish-feminist enterprise is dissenting from Jewish tradition, I see it as in line with the tradition; feminist interpretations of Judaism and feminist innovation in Jewish religious practice are within the bounds of the ancient Jewish tradition of innovation, questioning, and debate.

11

Reclaiming God

Ambiguity, Religion, and Faith

AZZA M. KARAM

"Please, please don't say anything negative or critical about Islam. It is your faith!"

Such were the words of my late mother, with whom my relationship was never the easiest. As I embarked upon the journey of studying the tensions in my part of the world—the Middle East—among religion, governance, and women's rights, her words remained with me as it became clear that these three issues were key in structuring the dynamics of our lives, whether in terms of local or global politics, social issues, or economics. Whether it was in our family or within the entire geographical region, religion, in this case Islam, was *it*. Suddenly, Islam, or people's versions of it, was becoming the single most important determinant of all decisions.

It took several years, as I worked with various organizations (local, regional, and international) on projects dealing with the extremely tricky subject of human rights, for me to begin to feel that it was inevitable that religious arguments would be the ones that all protagonists—whether those in rule or in opposition—would bandy about. Eventually, I came to ask why it was that women were so symbolic a terrain of contention in all these arguments, made largely by men.

"This is Islamic," shouted the activists promoting new changes in the Egyptian Family Laws that would give the wife with children the right to retain the apartment after she was divorced from her husband. Yet, "according to our Islamic tradition," a counterpoint against this same amendment would also be voiced. Even in one family, opposing viewpoints rang out, sometimes in a heated debate. Which perspective *is* Islamic? Why is "Islamic" so important anyway? Why do we not have such heated debates about what is Islamic when discussing the impact of World Bank and IMF

Structural Adjustment Policies, which force our government to cut subsidies, thereby making poor people unable to afford bread?

To my mother's plea (more like a command) I would in the beginning roll my eyes in mock anguish, thinking, "Honestly, Mother, why would Islamic faith be the issue in the first place?" After several years of listening to my mother's pleas, and further study on this issue, I ended up at one stage finding myself, in sheer frustration, raising my voice against my mother to articulate thoughts that had become clearer through my investigations and work on a variety of issues: "It is not about faith. It is not about faith at all. It is about a group of men—politicians, religious leaders, even notable NGO activists—dancing around with religion as nothing more than a tool. And it is a macabre ritual ultimately defaming our faith. Who says it belongs to them anyway? Is God not mine too?"

In the end my mother's warnings informed me more than any arguments, books, or even life experiences could or did. She was right, of course, in her own way, because none of what was going on in the domain of politics is really about the faith itself, instead, it concerns the fundamentals of religious politics that uses the tools of religion purely for political ends.

When I finally came to writing down the results of my study and work, I found myself devoting considerable time and energy at the very beginning to clarifying that not only was I *not* studying or referencing the Islamic faith, I was zeroing in on the phenomenon of the *politicization of religion* (see Karam 1998a, 1998b, 2004). The phenomenon involving the Islamic religion that I have called political Islam (or Islamism), I have continued to distinguish from institutionalized religious bodies (ministries, religious schools) and fundamentalism (which as a movement was not necessarily politically engaged or involved).

In short, I found myself searching for definitions that fit the situation I documented and saw developing all over the Middle East. None of the academic or practical paradigms seemed to address my questions. In fact, I was swimming against the current and losing friends from both the academic arena (where I was eventually involved in teaching) and the activist arena (my permanent dwelling and learning place). I realized that some academics, particularly Western ones, were far more comfortable, when dealing with my part of the world, with certain linguistic categories, such as fundamentalism, because otherwise complex phenomena could then be amenable to grouping (for example, Islamic fundamentalism as part of religious fundamentalism). Consequently, relatively simple theorization could then be carried out and presented as knowledge. Some of my activist colleagues, on the other hand, were equally attracted by this process of categorization—or naming—which gave "the opposition" a clearer garb (for example, "fundamentalism is antidemocratic and anti-women"), whereupon the strategy of attack became less convoluted and clearer. The resulting thought process goes thus: Islamic fundamentalism is antidemocratic and anti-women → Islamic fundamentalists are enemies of democracy and women's rights → therefore anyone arguing for Islam is against democracy and women's rights. So the activist and academic solution is to not engage with Islam, indeed with religion, at all. People, such as "non-democrats," cannot be engaged in the struggle for democracy. If you must have religion, then keep it personal, was the argument.

Something inside me revolted against both this logic and its rhetoric. On the one hand, to be a feminist is to maintain that the personal is political, a fact I believe wholeheartedly. But on the other hand, when it comes to faith, some of my academic friends and activists would have us maintain that it has to be "just personal." In other words, when it comes to faith, the personal is not political? I wondered. This query was particularly significant to me because I realized that by rendering faith nonpolitical and personal, one could not challenge what was taking place, in the name of religion, in the political arena. We were thus, even as feminists, participating in the act of silencing ourselves.

Those who speak in the name of religion do not do so personally; they create very public agendas of governance, economics, culture, and social interaction based on their understanding of what is religious. Millions are swayed by these agendas; indeed, millions vote on the basis of such religious agendas. Surely that voting is an act of democracy, so how can I afford not to engage? Do I become a non-democrat and exclude millions of people and what sways them, as my academic and activists friends suggested and did, in the name of fighting for democracy? These agendas only begin to outline the vast world of religion that I wanted spoken about so that better paradigms might be developed for the future of the Middle East.

Here again I found much resentment from colleagues and some friends. Those who felt more comfortable with the secular nomenclature felt I was too religious for their taste. I remember one of them looking at me worriedly and asking, in some shock, whether I had decided to "get veiled" (said most pejoratively). (I was wearing a relatively large headband to hold back my then long and unruly hair.) I remember being surprised, and even upset, not because I was mistaken for veiled, but because that seemed to cause so much consternation. So what if I decide to veil? If I chose to do it, would my human right to choice in this case not be acceptable to the same activists who claim fervently to uphold freedom of choice? And would they deny my right to choose because it originated in an ethic and a belief?

On the other hand, Islamist and even some conservative Muslims saw me as far too secular and even un-Islamic. Why? Because not only do I refuse to wear the veil (maintaining that modesty is not defined by what you hide of your physical body or form), but I still characterize myself as a believer. I am also critical of those who claim to understand the religion enough to let their understanding be the sole determinant of what constitutes and distinguishes between believer and infidel, between Islamic and non-Islamic.

To both sets of detractors, my response was this: Surely, if you believe in God, you must also believe that God alone is the judge of each and all of us? Surely, to believe is also to appreciate the verse in the Holy Qur'an that indicates that God created us in all our diversity, not that we should sit in judgment of each other, but that we should *know* one another? And again, I think, surely, to be a Muslim is to also read and learn that the term *Muslim* is used in the Holy Qur'an itself to refer to people who existed even before the advent of Islam as we know it today? Indeed, is it not used to refer to Abraham and consecutive prophets and people who were believers? At best, our faith is about tremendous inclusiveness. At worst, it should make us realize that nothing is clear cut, that everything bespeaks an ambiguity that in itself is a miracle of our creation and existence. Those, at least, are my beliefs.

My disillusionment with some of my fellow activists and academics prompted me to think that maybe the naming, oversimplified categorization, and exclusiveness were a function of the struggle for democracy in the Middle East itself, and that perhaps living in the so-called liberal and democratic West would enable me to be less of an anomaly. Years later, after living and working in the Netherlands, Sweden, and Northern Ireland, I felt I was beginning to understand the ways of the West. Plenty of diversity characterized every country and indeed every person I met, and yet, despite being as professionally integrated as possible (with a full-time job, a home, and a family), I felt alien to these cultures and ways of thinking. Naming and categorization was rampant here, too, but with a new addition: stereotyping. I was labeled a migrant or a foreigner; I could never be "of the country," for I was too different.

As a believer, I was considered stranger still. People wanted to know how I could be comfortable being a Muslim when Islam was "so oppressive toward women"—as the dominant stereotype depicts. I will never forget sitting through a radio interview in The Netherlands on the theme of Islam and women, wherein I maintained that my Islamic faith is my source of strength, and being told by the woman interviewer that "being so educated and still being a believer in Islam, surely, [I] was an exception [to Muslim society]."

Her statement left me feeling angry and even more disillusioned. It also opened the door to much introspection and analysis of Western thought. Why is it so ingrained, even in some of the supposedly enlightened and informed minds, that Islam, indeed religion, is oppressive? And why is it that to be a person of faith is to be so odd? In Sweden I had the opportunity to further my introspection and analysis by working specifically with democracy issues. I realized that the gulf between the secular and the religious often lay at the root of many of the disputes around democratization that were taking place in many parts of the world. Some would even go so far as to say that many of the wars were caused by religion. Once again I found myself asking questions: What is it about religion that can evoke so much negativity and misunderstanding? Why is there a dominant idea that to be religious is to be undemocratic, conflict-causing, and, in short, problematic?

By then I had also grown tired of believing that one could be what one wished to be in the liberal West. To be a person of faith, I thought, one was bound to be the "other," anywhere one was. In addition, at least one of the myriad others of my identity—Muslim-woman-Arab-educated-activist-teacher-living in the West—was always going to render me "other" in some place at some time. Far from making me doubt my faith, the varied processes of exclusion (whether by Arab secularists or religious people, by Western academic theorists or democracy activists, by neighbors and friends) made me realize precisely why it was that faith was central and important. To question being a woman of faith was to question each and every other aspect of my identity, and whereas that will always be part of existing—for no aspect of identity should ever be taken for granted—it is precisely because of the faith that each dimension makes sense as part of a whole. Faith is not about exclusion but about inclusion.

To believe in God is to believe that somewhere human avarice, cruelty, judgmentalism, exclusion, and the pain encountered in different parts of the world, are not the norm. Indeed, to believe in God is to realize that there is a countervailing force that also provides the self-same humans with empathy, kindness, and the most healing of all powers, love. To me, to be a Muslim is to realize that diversity (within and outside of us) is part of the wonder of being. I could not be all that I am without my faith. This was taught to me by another remarkable woman who had herself encountered, in her own society, many forms of exclusion and bitterness. Mia Berden, my Dutch Christian mentor, literally and figuratively held my hand through the rough times and showed me how it was that faith was the art of love, the bearer of courage, and the means of survival through connectedness with other people of faith.

I came to the United States in the winter of 2000 specifically to work with multiple communities of faith. I believe it was God's guidance that enabled me come to a country that I have held in such fascination for many, many years, and one that, ironically, despite finding its foreign policy at times abhorrent, I was nevertheless deeply attracted to. Why? Because it represents precisely the diversity that I find so Islamic. I have often heard it repeated that the United States is a country of immigrants from all over the world. Compared to Western Europe (with the exception of the United Kingdom), the diversity in the United States is certainly more pronounced and bound to influence the way its culture is formulated and changing. After living in New York City and working with different religious and academic communities around the country nearly the same number of years as I have lived and worked in several other Western European countries, I do not find my multiple identities problematic. Nor indeed am I finding that being a woman of faith is leading to painful processes of "othering." Fortunately, my work takes me to many parts of the United States and to other countries, as well as allowing me to mingle with varied communities of faith, features that may have facilitated the fact that both my stay in the United States and the nature of those I have been blessed to work with are in sync with my character. Needless to say, the fact that a good deal of discrimination and stereotyping of different communities exist in the midst of this diversity renders this a less than perfect society. Nevertheless, looking at things from a comparative perspective, I believe that being a society built on diversity, the capacity for acceptance (or at least for a "live and let live" attitude) of people of faith and of multiple identities is not only a potential but a reality in the United States.

It is a big pitfall to render religion the only "right" in a world of "wrongs," an action that brings the consequent slide into religious righteousness that we so often hear and see among the Religious Right emergent in some communities in certain countries in the Middle East (Iran, Saudi Arabia, Israel), Europe (Kosovo, Bosnia), South Asia (India, Pakistan, Afghanistan), and North America (the United States). But much of the politics of righteousness, whether religious or secular, is built on exclusion, or what I refer to as the politics of "othering," intimately connected to dualistic thinking (right vs. wrong, black vs. white, good vs. bad, us vs. them). But being a person of faith, as I indicated earlier, means also realizing that the dividing line between communities and/or peoples is not so clear cut, and that being different in our creeds, race, gender, and whatever else is what makes our existence richer—if more complicated. Ambiguity is not easy to contend with, but it is the essence of our lives, and fundamentally why we need faith. Faith seeks to be creative with the ambiguous materials of our lives; it provides a framework, adds nuance to meanings, and often provides colors to what others would have us believe is only black and white.

In my studies of women of faith and their many works representing different religious traditions, and in working with communities of faith, several realities became apparent to me. Not only are women of faith the bulwark of faith-based services—forming, in some instances, over 90 percent of basic service providers in religious communities—but, whether Traditional African, Chinese, Buddhist, Hindu, Jewish, Christian, Muslim, or Baha'i, these women of faith see a huge difference between the spirit of their faith and the practices done in the name of their religion. Many of these women, through their remarkable intellectual endeavors and activism in both public and private domains, seek to reclaim their religious heritage and reinterpret the understandings of religion such that the faith becomes central to practice rather than the all-too-common current paradigm, where the religious institution is the focus of the practice and its sole interpreter. Part of the significance of their faith-work is the affirmation of the fact that far from being solely a tool of women's oppression, religion is a fundamental aspect of the struggle for human emancipation, and with it, for women's rights. There is no way that this process of reclaiming the religious can take place by ignoring religion and castigating or alienating those who would speak in its name, or indeed, assuming that only the religious institutions represent the "religious."

During one of my work trips to Peru to launch the Latin American and Caribbean sub-network of women of faith (as part of my organization's Global Network of Religious Women's Organizations), I vividly remember a visit to a home run by nuns. The home was tailored for "vulnerable" women, those who had suffered the vagaries of life (at least 25 percent of the 100 plus women in the home, ranging in age from twelve to twenty-two, were single mothers, and had become such at the age of fourteen). The women were from all over the country. Far from following the institutional line of confession followed by marginalization from society, the nuns' philosophy was to empower the young women to enable them to look after themselves, to be proud of their children and their achievements as mothers, and to be able to face society with heads held high with the pride and humility that only a liberating faith can engender. These young women were not only clearly happy to be where they were, but they were keen that we visitors (largely a group of multireligious women from other parts of the South American continent) see their children and their varied handiwork. Far from shying away from other religious women, they were comfortable enough with faith to want to know more about the diverse traditions of the religious women they were visited by. I left that home with an impression of laughter, of strength, and a strong sense of faith as empowering, and women of faith as part of the process of coming back to life after much pain.

A similar experience was voiced in one of our workshops on women, religion and conflict through a story narrated by a Christian Palestinian living as a citizen of Israel. She spoke about a Jewish woman of faith, also in Israel. In a crowded street in Jerusalem, our participant shared, this Orthodox Jewish woman threw herself over a Muslim youth to protect him from a physical onslaught by some Jewish youth. Physical contact between women and men—strangers—is frowned upon by Orthodox Jews, our participant explained (not unlike the disapproval by both Christians and Muslims in various Islamic cultures). And yet, this Observant Jewish Orthodox woman of faith broke that "contact taboo" to protect a young boy who was not only from another faith tradition but also from what was ostensibly an "enemy" community. The Orthodox Jewish woman was not seeing the differences and lines of enmity that separated the communities; instead, she reacted out of her concern for a fellow human being, and out of her conviction and faith. The Palestinian woman who narrated this story concluded by sharing how deeply this action had affected her and changed much of her perception of the possibilities of coexistence between the two communities: Palestinians (both Christian and Muslim) and Israelis.

My life in the Middle East taught me that to be a believer in human rights, in democracy, and in feminism (which encompasses both and much else), I had to reclaim the domain of the religious as part of my struggle to understand myself and my society—an understanding that no politician, caught in the web of fighting for political power, in the midst of conflicting ideals, would be able to explain. My life in the West thus far has taught me that I must reclaim faith to appreciate the diversity I am in the midst of as part of the wonder of my own religious tradition, which includes an appreciation of the wonders of any religious faith—a wonder that no religious clergy, experienced in fighting for a specific domain of political or religious power in a peculiar context at a certain moment of time, would be able to articulate. Both experiences have also brought me to the realization that one can be religious and a feminist at the same time. Religious feminism is not merely a concept but a reality borne of the joint struggles of women of faith for their rights within their faith.

Faith is like life. It has its ambiguities and its certainties, and, depending on where one stands, one sees the specific dimensions one wishes to acknowledge. One can choose, as I do, to live life based on and with faith. As with life, faith will continue to baffle and illuminate, thwart and enable, mystify and empower. But, also like life, it is unavoidable . . . and necessary.

12

From Center to Margin:
A Feminist Journey
in the Roman Catholic Church

A Socio-religious Approach
to Autobiography

SUSAN A. FARRELL

INTRODUCTION

Writing now from a perspective informed by a sociological framework, I see my life through what C. Wright Mills termed the "lens of the sociological imagination." Our individual lives are interconnected and shaped by the social and economic forces of the times in which we live. And so my brief autobiographical story written for this book takes shape within a family and a society shaped by post–World War II America. For me, it is important to note the people in my life who helped shape what I call my feminist spirituality. My spirituality remains rooted in the Roman Catholic faith—a faith that is "the assurance of things hoped for, the conviction of things not seen" (Heb 11:1). My Roman Catholic faith has been enriched by my feminist spirituality. Feminist theologians such as Elisabeth Schüssler Fiorenza, Rosemary Radford Ruether, Beverly Wildung Harrison, Carter Heyward, Mary Hunt, Mary I. Buckley, and many others too numerous to mention here, have touched my life both through their writing and contact with them at conferences and in the Women-Church Convergence, a feminist Roman Catholic group of which I'll speak of later. Blessedly, some of these women I can also speak of as friends.

As an unapologetic academic, I believe that ideas expressed in literature and research can nourish life as well as religious and theological writing.

The intellectual life for me is an integral part of my spirituality. But I also see teaching as activism, and this too is informed by my faith. Dietrich Bonhoeffer (1906–45), a German pastor in the Confessing Church who gave his life resisting Hitler, said that faith is not passive; it is activism. I agree and find my faith, my spirituality, my research, and my activist teaching intersecting in mutually supportive ways. Many would find a Roman Catholic faith and feminism to be contradictory, but neither I nor those Catholic feminists with whom I study and work agree with that view. For us, the values espoused by Jesus and the early Christian church are very much about justice, equality, and love. What does contradict these values is the patriarchy and structures of inequality in the institutional church.

As a sociologist, I research and analyze the organizational church; as a feminist Roman Catholic, I, with the women and men of Women-Church and other progressive Roman Catholic organizations, work for the transformation of a religious organization from a patriarchal structure to an egalitarian one. We are convinced by our faith that, although unseen as yet in its fullness, the church can become an inclusive institution. So we embody the activist faith of Bonhoeffer and stand on the prophetic margins of the church calling for and working for "new women, new church, new priestly ministry" (motto of the Women's Ordination Conference).

SPIRITUAL ROOTS AND RELIGIOUS TRAINING

My mother used to joke that she had bail money saved for me in case I should ever be arrested in a civil rights demonstration. I was never arrested, and the bail money was not needed. But the activist Roman Catholic religious order I entered in 1967, the Daughters of Wisdom, seemed a natural continuation of my parents' own commitment to social justice. Members of the NAACP, my parents believed strongly in equality and raised their children with an awareness of the terrible racial injustices in America. Their belief in equality grew out of their belief in American democracy and their Roman Catholicism. My father, though, was a convert from Presbyterianism. Perhaps this was why I was drawn to Bonhoeffer's life and theology as filtered through my father's very different take on Catholicism in contrast to my mother, who was an Irish-German American cradle Catholic. My father was always questioning Roman Catholicism, and so he readily accepted and engaged in the changes brought about by the Second Vatican Council. Dad had the kind of critical analytic mind that we sociologists try so hard to instill in our students. He handed this sociological perspective on to me before I even knew what sociology was. My spiritual journey combines both the traditionalism of my mother and the somewhat unorthodox views of my father with their deep sense of social justice. This commitment to social justice was deepened by my experience with the Daughters of Wisdom.

Although I was only in the Daughters of Wisdom for a scant two years, the experience profoundly shaped the rest of my life. Founded in France in 1704 by Saint Louis Marie De Monfort and Blessed Marie Louise Trichet, the Daughters of Wisdom believed they had a mission to educate young people and care for the sick. Their work was primarily to the poor, although later it was extended to the growing middle classes of Canada, the United States, and to the French colonies in Haiti and Africa. I went to high school at Our Lady of Wisdom Academy in Ozone Park, Queens, New York, where the sisters taught. After my four years of high school with them, I decided to enter the order. Ever since I could remember, I had wanted to be a nun. I wanted to be one of those women dedicated to Christ and the church, and I wanted to teach. Those were my two ambitions in life.

It was a life in some ways similar to that of a young woman depicted in a semi-autobiographical story by Simone de Beauvoir (1908–86), an existentialist philosopher, feminist, and friend and lover of Jean-Paul Sartre. De Beauvoir is best known for the feminist classic *The Second Sex* (1949). In *When Things of the Spirit Come First* (1979) she describes a pious childhood filled with longing for mystical experiences. Mine was similar, although much later, in the 1950s. I wanted to and aimed to be a good Catholic girl with a life filled with all the small pieties taught to us by the nuns. I went to Catholic grammar and high school. I went frequently to weekday mass as well as Sunday mass, often accompanying my grandmother in the wee hours of the morning, especially during Lent. We also went to the Stations of the Cross on Fridays in that penitential season and to Benediction throughout the rest of the year. I had prayer books and statues of my favorite saints in my bedroom and even was the proud possessor of a holy-card collection. Much of this was shared with my cousin, who would later go on to become a priest. He has remained in the priesthood, a conservative and truly pastoral man. My journey has gone in a different direction although still profoundly shaped by these early socialization patterns.

From such beginnings, with a good dose of social justice concerns added, I emerged from the convent in 1970 unsure of what I wanted to do. I had pinned all my desires on living a life of service to God, of teaching in that service. But both the novice mistress and I decided that this was not the life for me. I had no problem with either poverty or chastity, but obedience was not a strong character trait. I questioned too much and even in those more liberal times for religious orders, obedience was still important in the formation of young nuns.

Now what? Vatican II was just over, and I decided to take up the liberal causes of the church and society. I became immersed in the local parish life in which my parents were also active. Active involvement in the life of the church was now possible for lay people. Beyond decorating altars and belonging to the Holy Name Society, lay people could become lectors, eucharistic ministers, and parish leaders. My father was president of the parish council and took the new opportunities opened to him by Vatican II very seriously. From his perspective, this was simply Catholics coming around to the way Protestants did things. I happily joined the committee on liturgy hoping to bring all the knowledge gained from my convent education to my parish, which was still hesitant about church reforms.

But the parish went slowly, too slowly for someone who was already receiving communion in the hand and under two species (bread and wine) in the convent. As I headed back to college, I was slowly becoming disillusioned with parish life. Universities in 1969 and 1970 were still the epicenters of the antiwar movement, and I joined in with eagerness and determination. I attended Queens College of the City University of New York. Social justice issues were at the top of the required reading lists in almost all courses. May 1970 brought the tragedies of Kent State and Jackson State universities. As with many others in my generation, Vietnam, the peace movement, and the student movement intersected with the civil rights movement to raise consciousness and conscience about injustices in the United States and the world. It would require one more crucial event in my life to move me into yet another social justice movement: meeting the man who would become my life's partner. My spiritual life was and is more complete because of our relationship. We talked about having children and what our life would be like after we had them. He remarked that of course I'd finish school and go out to work. My mother had never worked outside the home once she had children. But Edward's mother had, and that's the example with which he grew up. I spent some time thinking about this as I raised two small children.

TOWARD A FEMINIST SPIRITUALITY

We and a few close friends attended weekly mass at St. John's, my husband's alma mater. It was a welcoming place for children and adults seeking a more intimate liturgical and worship community than could be had in many parishes even after Vatican II. At Edward's suggestion I enrolled for a summer institute at St. John's University in Queens. I was still interested in religious and theological issues. This institute would turn out to be the first feminist theological conference in the United States.

That conference created in me a still developing feminist consciousness and conscience which, for me, encompass and support all other social justice causes. Hearing feminist theologians and ethicists such as Elisabeth Schüssler Fiorenza, Mary Buckley, Carter Heyward, and Beverly Harrison excited and engaged me in a another social movement for change. I began reading everything these women and others were writing. Rosemary Radford Ruether's *New Woman/New Earth* (1975), along with *Womanspirit Rising,* edited by Carol Christ and Judith Plaskow (1979), now feminist theological classics, then served to open up questions and critiques of patriarchal religion.

Feminism is now the heart and soul of my spiritual life, but of itself, feminism did not move me from the Catholic Church. I decided to return to college for a master's degree in theology, still determined to work in the church, still dreaming of service to the church. One of my professors, Dr. Mary Buckley, who had organized that first feminist theology conference, expressed some concern about my choice of careers. She wanted to know what my husband did for a living. Did he too work for the church in some capacity? "No," I answered. "Good," she replied. "Someone has to have a real job." Church-related careers, now, as ever, do not pay well, either for women or men although men are better paid, as in all economic sectors.

I soon had a job teaching religious studies to high school students in a Catholic high school in Queens, New York. My favorite course was "Women in the World," which I taught to the senior girls. My second-favorite course was a course on moral issues for the juniors. Because of my involvement with this course, I was invited to be a member of the Northeast Feminist Ethics Consultation by Dr. Beverly Harrison, then a professor of Christian ethics at Union Theological Seminary. She had been a friend since the second summer institute at St. John's University in 1980, where she gave a lecture on family and feminism. Involvement with the Feminist Ethicists Consultation laid the groundwork for my continued work in the area of sexual ethics and feminism. This interest in feminism, religion, and sexual ethics would become the basis for my doctoral dissertation as well.

MOVING TOWARD THE MARGINS

My commitment to social justice was tested in 1983 when my union went on strike. The Lay Faculty Union was a small unit that had organized the teachers at several Catholic highs schools in Brooklyn and Queens. My high school, St. John's Preparatory High School, was formerly a diocesan high school in Brooklyn, meaning that it was run by the diocese for students from the geographical area in which it was located, in this case, Astoria, Queens. But at this time dioceses all over the United States were divesting their Catholic schools and setting them up as independent regional high schools with Catholic lay boards comprised of parents and local business people. St. John's Prep, formerly Mater Christi, went a slightly different route. Close to St. John's University in Queens, the schools decided to work together, with the prep becoming a feeder school for the university. This would benefit both the university and the high school. The high school would gain the prestige of being connected with the university and the university could more easily recruit students from the local area.

There was, however, one problem. Several years earlier, St. John's University had broken its union through a long and difficult strike. If our small union succeeded in negotiating a good contract, long-time high-school faculty with tenure would be making more than the college professors. The board, composed of some members of the university and some local business people, did not want to give those raises, nor did it want a union at the high school. In addition, the board demanded that pregnant women resign their faculty positions. Although labor law states that pregnant women cannot be fired or laid off, this in essence was what the board wanted to do. Strange and contradictory actions from a school affiliated with a religion that believes a woman's ultimate vocation is to marry and bear children, as Pope John Paul II so clearly stated in his encyclical letter "On the Dignity and Vocation of Women" (*Dignitatis mulieris*, 1988).

Although this union-busting activity flew in the face of Catholic social justice teaching (see encyclicals by Leo XIII and John Paul II), the board decided to break the union. Those of us on strike were replaced with scabs. I was devastated. One of the board members was chaplain at St. John's University. We attended this worship community every Sunday. My children received first communion there. My husband had received his BA from the university. I had my MA in theology from St. John's. We taught Sunday school there, and I was a eucharistic minister for the community. I gave out communion side by side with this board member, a Vincentian priest, along with other Vincentians who also taught my theology classes as well as ministered in that community. When I asked him to intervene in this dispute, his reply was simply this: "Susan, I know that you are a good Catholic woman, but there is nothing I can do." This priest, as well as others in that community, would often participate in grape and lettuce boycotts for the farm workers, but when it came to injustice in his own backyard, he couldn't or wouldn't see it.

My faith was strongly connected to a sense of justice and equality. Starting with those early commitments to civil rights and then feminism, I really could not believe in a church that treated people unjustly. This union contract dispute was connected with feminism, because of the demand that pregnant women must resign their teaching positions or be laid off. How could an organization identified with Roman Catholicism punish women for being pregnant? I came to understand that this church to which I belonged was testing my faith. For my faith to survive, I had to remove myself from the organizational structure. My family and I left the St. John's University Sunday Community. We could not worship with people whose sense of social justice disappeared with the bottom line. I also no longer had a job. So, at my husband's suggestion, I went back to school. Disillusioned with Catholic theological teaching and seeing its real limitations for women, I returned to school for women's studies. Not being able to travel beyond the New York area, I applied to the City University of New York's graduate school, where I would major in sociology and take a certificate in women's studies.

RESEARCH: FEMINISM, WOMEN-CHURCH, AND THE ROMAN CATHOLIC CHURCH

Traditionally, graduate students are advised to do their dissertations on subjects with which they are familiar. I was no different. My advisors knew of my background in Roman Catholicism and interest in religion. They encouraged me to do research on women in the Roman Catholic Church. My work did provoke some discussion among the members of my dissertation committee. The three women who constituted this committee were all Jewish, each one representing a place along the continuum of believing and belonging. In fact, one felt the dissertation might be irrelevant in the near future, because any feminist woman would finally come to her senses and leave such a patriarchal institution. I disagreed, and the four of us explored why feminists would remain believing in and belonging to the Roman Catholic Church. Since I was already active in the Women's Ordination Conference (WOC) and some other feminist Catholic groups, I decided to study Women-Church. Women-Church is not one organization but a coalition of autonomous feminist groups and organizations rooted in the Roman Catholic Church and tradition. The group's formal name is the Women-Church Convergence. Its primary goal is the ordination of women as full Roman Catholic priests with the rights to move up the church hierarchy and to participate in church governance, including at the Vatican.

The first meeting was held in Chicago in 1983 with fifteen hundred people in attendance. Originally a movement with great support among religious communities, laywomen are now the majority. The organization is also ecumenical and has grown in numbers and scope. The organization consists of approximately thirty-five groups. Some of these groups are quite large, for example, the WOC and several religious orders with hundreds of members. Groups such as the Women's Alliance for Theology, Ethics, and Ritual (commonly called WATER) are medium-sized organizations operating on a local level but with international ties to similar groups in Latin America and Europe.

Other participating organizations include Catholics for a Free Choice, with international partners in Latin America and Europe. This organization was founded to promote procreative choice for Catholic women and men. Other members are small parish groups of women or grassroots Women-Church groups from particular geographical locations. Selected members of each of these groups serve on the steering committee of the Women-Church Convergence. If an individual is a member of any of these organizations, that person is also a member of Women-Church. These are women who do not want to leave the church but are determined to change the church.

Women-Church has made connections with Catholic social justice groups such as Call to Action (a Catholic lay group whose aim is to democratize the church), and the Center for Concern and the Quixote Center (which focus on Catholic concerns over U.S. involvement in Central and South America linking religious liberation movements with political liberation). Links have also been forged with CORPUS (an organization that supports married priests). Members of DIGNITY (an organization of gay and lesbian Catholics) also participate in Women-Church. Most important, many religious orders remain active both through participation and by making resources available for Women-Church. Association with Las Hermanas (a Catholic Hispanic women's group) extends the coalition beyond U.S. borders. Women-Church Convergence members support and participate in Women's Ordination

Worldwide (WOW), a global network of organizations that support the ordination of women in the Roman Catholic Church.

Women-Church, then, is a social movement seeking to change church ideology. It presents an alternative model for being church as it challenges the present institutional arrangements that exclude women as well as laymen from positions of authority. The Women-Church Convergence sees itself as "raising a feminist voice and committed to an *ekklesia* [church] of women which is participative, egalitarian and self-governing." It is working "to eradicate patriarchy, especially sexism and racism, in order to transform church and society" (Women-Church Convergence website).

I've been studying Women-Church now for twenty years as an "insider-outsider" in Robert K. Merton's sense of the researcher who studies what he or she is a part of, otherwise known as a "participant-observer" (Merton 1972). I'm a member of some of the organizations that make up the Women-Church Convergence, and the convergence steering committee has allowed me to sit in on its board meetings for my research. In my articles and papers I have analyzed Women-Church as it has grown and changed strategies for transforming the Roman Catholic Church. I have interviewed leaders and members of Women-Church to find out how feminist Roman Catholic women live with the tension between their beliefs and the teachings of the official church. I also have analyzed the publications of Women-Church and the organization's members as a way of comparing and contrasting their beliefs and practices with official church teaching. The contrast is most pronounced on two issues: the ordination of women and sexual issues, notably abortion, contraception, premarital sex, and homosexuality.

Women-Church stands in the liberal tradition of reform movements in the Roman Catholic Church. Throughout the church's history there has been a tension between liberal and conservative groups. In the aftermath of Vatican II two distinct groups emerged in a struggle for power and authority in the church. Conservatives wanted a return to the pre–Vatican II church with power consolidated in the clergy and the Curia. Liberals wanted to continue Vatican II reforms and shift power to the laity and the local churches. This struggle mirrors the conflicts experienced in almost all contemporary religious traditions.

The last few decades have seen a rise in religious fundamentalism and a corresponding resistance and challenge by liberals and modernists. Women-Church is a case study in how a liberal group both challenges traditional religious authority and counters conservative movements within its own tradition and the world at large. Aligned with the secular women's movement, Women-Church asserts the rights of women to participate fully in all social institutions. It opposes any group that is attempting to diminish those rights already won, such as procreative choice, and continues to work for the transformation of the church and other institutions that do not yet grant full rights to women. In light of the conflict between Women-Church beliefs and official church teachings, I've concluded that Women-Church is creating an oppositional discourse with the aim of constructing a new understanding of gender and sexual ethics in the church.

Interviews with members of Women-Church support this conclusion. Over and over, these women insist that they do not and will not leave the church— meaning the people of God. They often remind me that the church is not the institution but a community of believers. They quote Vatican II's *Pastoral Constitution on the Church in the Modern World (Gaudium et spes):*

> Where they have not yet won it, women claim for themselves an equity with men before the law and in fact. . . . With respect to the fundamental rights of the person, every type of discrimination, whether social or cultural, whether based on sex, race, color, social condition, language, or religion, is to be overcome and eradicated as contrary to God's intent. (*GS*, nos. 9, 29)

Women and men I've interviewed tell me that the church should practice what it has declared in this document; it should treat women equally, which, for them, means ordaining women.

One interviewee and scholar who has written on women's ordination, Mary Buckley, often stated that if women cannot be ordained, then this means that they are not fully redeemed either. She bases this on the belief that baptism, for Roman Catholics, is the sacrament that initiates and allows the reception of the other six sacraments: Eucharist, reconciliation, confirmation, matrimony, the sacrament for the sick and dying, and holy orders. But women who are baptized still cannot be ordained. Buckley concludes that women's baptism must somehow be incomplete or suspect. In fact, she reminded me that the Council of Trent (1545–63) was not totally sure that women had souls, so their redemption was indeed questionable. Regardless of what doubts male leadership of the church may have about women, the women of Women-Church continue to say that "it's our church, too," and they have no intentions of leaving.

THE FUTURE OF WOMEN-CHURCH

I've expanded my interviews to include young Catholic adults as well as veterans of the feminist movement in the church. To the question, Why remain in the church, especially when so many young people are either nonreligious or uncommitted to any organized religion or tend to be more conservative? all agreed with one young woman's statement: "If I'm not there, who will be the liberal voice in the church?" This is a very similar response to other feminists in the church of whom I've asked the same question. Further, all these young people also believe in the Vatican II message that they are church. They heard this message loud and clear through their socialization into this post–Vatican II church despite reactionary voices from the hierarchy.

Their generational identity came through when another young woman voiced concern over "the slowness of the older generation," as she put it, "to confront the bishops." "Enough talking," she said, " let's just get on with it." Another young woman also lamented the constant rehashing of old conflicts either with the hierarchy or within the feminist groups themselves. She said that she heard enough about what happened in WOC or the Women-Church Convergence twenty years ago. Let it go and move forward. "New leadership is needed and it's time for older members to let go and for younger people to move up," she said.

There seems to be both an impatience to get on with the feminist movement and yet a search for strategies that have yet to be developed. Some of the younger members felt that older leaders and members couldn't quite let go because they did not trust the younger members with the movement and the organization. This seemed to be echoed in both the Women-Church organizations and DIGNITY. One thing that came across to me most clearly in these interviews and focus groups is that if these feminist and progressive organizations don't start making room for and inviting young women and men into leadership positions, these young adults will find the organizations increasingly irrelevant to them and to the world in which they live.

CONCLUSION: LIFE ON THE MARGINS

These feminist organizations and their members live, as I do, on the margins of the Roman Catholicism. But many feel that it is their faith that gives them the strength to use the margin as a prophetic stance. If they leave completely, as the radical post-Christian feminist Mary Daly and countless others have, then the institution does not have to take them seriously. If they stay, albeit on the margins, they remain engaged in the discourse of challenge and transformation. Life on the margins is not easy, and it is filled with tension. One of the leaders of a Women-Church organization said that she felt that "it's not a question of 'if' I leave but 'when.' But I'll stay at least until you've finished your book."

And for the moment, that is where I stand, too. My research and my faith life intersect here as I work with Women-Church to create what is yet unseen but hoped for: a church in which "there is no longer Jew and Greek, there is no longer slave and free, there is no longer male and female; for all of you are one in Christ Jesus" (Gal 3:28).

Epilogue

The Answering Word

VICTORIA LEE ERICKSON
and SUSAN A. FARRELL

The *anticipated word* found in our chapters deserves an *answering word*, a life-giving response. These chapters deserve a conversation that does not end here. Interestingly enough, we knew this on Monday, May 5, 2003. Looking back, this book project owes more than we could have imagined to Nurah Ammat'ullah, MLIS, GC, who asked the editors to allow her to launch the book project as the central theme for the Second Annual Conference of the Muslim Women's Institute for Research and Development (MWIRD) held at the Kellogg Conference Center, International and Public Affairs Building, Columbia University, New York City, on Sunday, May 4, and Monday, May 5, 2003.

In attendance were members of MWIRD and its constituent communities, members of the Columbia University community, and several authors from the *Still Believing after All These Years* book project: Dr. Victoria Erickson, Dr. Susan Farrell, Dr. Rhonda Jacobsen, Dr. Anna Karpathakis, Dr. Judith Lorber, and Dr. Mira Morgenstern. Sunday we met for a shared meal and an evening plenary discussion where we heard papers on the subject "why we still believe after all these years." Monday we gathered again in three plenaries: In the morning we discussed "how is it that we should speak about each other in public and private conversations—how do the other members of the Abrahamic Family want to be understood?" In the afternoon we discussed what an Abrahamic interfaith dialogue between academic women might look like. Dr. Katharine Rhodes Henderson moderated a final session on "where we go from here."*

---

* The book project and conference members all lamented the shortage of Muslim women scholars available for the book project. A number declined, stating that they would have loved to have participated but their schedules were so demanding that they needed extended advanced notice to create the time necessary to write. We promised to include them in any future events.

131

When Dr. Henderson asked the group what had been accomplished, we announced that we were so impressed with the spirituality of Mira Morgenstern that we wanted to vote to make her our group's "rabbi." As Mira was speechless and blushing, her new Muslim friend, Nurah Ammat'ullah, asked her if we could all come to her house for a model Passover Seder. This is something, she said, she could do for us—providing that we came to her home knowing that children were at the center of the Seder's teaching goals. We all laughed; when it came to Jewish traditions, we all had the knowledge of children. And then, we thought that gathering during Ramadan and Epiphany would help the others understand Islam and Christianity. At the end of the conference we had decided that "what came next" was an intentional effort to form relationships that educated each other about each other as we enjoyed each other. The authors that could not attend the conference due to prior engagements regretted the schedule conflicts and asked to be put on the list for the Passover Seder so that they could also help plan future events.

The conference allowed us to share our first drafts of several of the book chapters you now hold in your hands. We asked one another questions and clarified our vocabularies. As we continued to write and rewrite over the year, the memory of this event shaped our thinking. We wrote with a realistic picture of each other, our students, and our communities in mind. It may be interesting for the reader to know that this educationally and spiritually wonderful experience might not have happened. Typically, academicians do not present their unpublished works-in-progress in a public forum like this, and it took us several weeks to decide whether or not to participate in the conference. What brought our participation about was MWIRD's plea; according to the director, "our women need to feel that they are invited at the beginning of a project and that their voices are important to the academic project, and they need to know that they have been heard." Muslim women from Harlem, the Caribbean, Africa, and perhaps other places from afar, were in attendance. It is our sincere effort here to respond to questions about ourselves, the way we think, and the reasons we "still believe" as we incorporate the voices of the conference attendees into our *answering word*.

Here in the Epilogue is at least an initial assessment of our words. Please remember that editors arrange books in ways that increase the teaching capacity of the text. Our chapters are arranged here from "the black and white of it" in Part I, where it is clear that believing and belonging produce long legacies of faith, to the "gray shades" of Part II, wherein authors discuss the problematic nature of both believing and belonging in ways not incongruent with Part 1, but that help us understand the reasons why some people decide not to believe or belong. Part III finds the heat turned up in the lives of our authors still more. We will let the reader decide what colors it brings to the text as authors take on issues of exclusion and violence precipitated by both religion and its enemies (these references are also present in Parts I and II) in the real-life struggle for peace and well-being among people. From the beginning to the end of this book, the reader will find these women of science to be living treasure boxes filled with the gifts that are ours when we believe, or when we solve the paradoxes of faith into an act of belonging to a community that claims us as one of its own.

PART I: A LEGACY OF BELIEVING

Although true of other others as well, in this section authors Duffy, Temple, and Ammat'ullah provide especially poignant narratives that point to the deep reservoir of faith that is available to them as an inheritance given by family and faith community. All three found themselves searching to experience not just the tradition's God but their God. Duffy and Temple remain in the Catholic and Protestant worlds of their families of origin; Ammat'ullah converts to Islam, where she finds her childhood conversations with Allah continued. All three are committed to making contributions to missions, to active charity in a world that needs them. All three find that their traditions provide strength of purpose in a fragile world in which human bonds require ongoing care-taking.

These Christian and Muslim women discovered that sharing the gifts of nature, art, music, and cultural resources with others brings spiritual renewal, creativity, and vision. For Duffy, her spiritual life empowers her publishing in science and spirituality and her work in the emerging science and religion dialogue—allowing her to sit on the board of directors of both the Metanexus Institute for Religion and Science and the American Teilhard Association. For Temple, her work in the biology laboratory and on the organist's bench unites the many creative energies of the mind, allowing her to become simultaneously both teacher and student of science and music. She sees herself as both storyteller of and character in the stories of religion and science. This co-creative and dialogical reality between science and religion allows her to see yet other ways to teach the methods of co-producing science with her students in their shared research projects in molecular biology and biochemistry. For Ammat'ullah, the gifts of science and faith drew her toward the community as she created a research agenda with them. A world traveler, Ammat'ullah brings the message of oneness not only to her clients in the Bronx but also to international venues where she advocates the uniting of the heart and the mind. Her efforts to bring immigrant and marginalized Muslim life to the academy are profoundly attached to the rich heritage of the educated Islamic mind. She seeks a true *ummah*, a true transcendence of ethnic and political differences.

Belief and their own believing in God, the great gifts of the Holy, and the community of faith are simply assumed by these authors as elemental building blocks of life, even life's foundation. Belief as a naturally occurring, lovely, and desirable quality of life allows them to be puzzled by those people who wonder and ask, "why do you still believe after all these years?" In the words of Temple, "Why not?" Why not, indeed? Believing and belonging have brought to them not only laughter and love but also difficult and mind-bending challenges to produce healing—scientific, political, cultural and sociological discoveries, changes, and new directions—in a world that needs their educated minds and hearts.

PART II: THE REWARDS OF BELONGING

The subject of believing and belonging becomes more complicated as these authors find many stumbling blocks to both. Professor Ochs finds that her believing has had little to do with certainty about God and everything to do with her belonging to a faith community. When people struggle with the truth about God or religion, claiming that they don't believe because of these dilemmas, she finds her very identity as a member of the Jewish community as "real," as what she needs to keep the faith. She is very much like her evangelical Christian colleague Dr. Jacobsen; both challenge detractors by arguing that there is more to religion than truth-claims. Although they tend to repress the negative aspects of their experiences in favor of a sustained belonging to their people, both see their traditions as crying out for change. Neither one believes that ignoring the gifts and leadership roles of women were right in the past or are right for the future. They see welcomed changes in Jewish and evangelical Christian communities. However, both stand with their communities against the disgust of others who unfairly judge their worthiness. Their academic wisdom allows them to challenge both their people and their enemies to ask better questions. Their critical scholarship keeps them believing in the value of their religious traditions, and their faith keeps them on the critical edge of science. Jacobsen speaks for Ochs, Lorber, and Karpathakis when she states that faith is not about being the guardian of how people should believe, it is about acting, and helping others act, to make this wonderfully complex world a good one to inhabit.

Professors Karpathakis and Lorber increase the complexity of faith stories. An astute sociologist of ethnicity and immigration, Karpathakis discusses the complexities of being born into an ethno-confessional group in which the secular and the religious are complexly intertwined and the answers to the question "Do I believe or do I belong?" are neither easy nor simple. One enters an ethnic group by birth, and the issues become increasingly complex when that ethnic group is also defined by a particular religion. Karpathakis's essay explores these complexities in relation to her own group, the Greek Orthodox. Lorber does not believe but finds comfort in belonging to a faith community. For the sake of their sons, both women seek the resources of the faith community. Karpathakis's story is one of coming to faith through her Greek grandmother, who read Bible stories to her that stretched her mind. Her grandmother expected answers to the creative and simple questions she asked her granddaughter about Jesus. By age ten, Karpathakis knew the stories of faith and the symbolism of the Greek Orthodox church. Finding the truth value of any of these difficult to ascertain, Karpathakis holds on to prayer. Professor Lorber tells us a similar story. She is drawn to the synagogue upon the death of her friend, to say *kaddish*, a prayer for the dead—to a God she does not believe in. She solves the paradox of faith through corporate prayer, a symbol of communal care giving.

After their many years in the academy and women's circles, the editors find Lorber's chapter a true gem, a loving testimony to the healing power of the gathered community of faith. Lorber tells us that she learned feminism and religion on her own, with little help from anyone. Her pioneering work in the sociology of medicine and of gender has won her great acclaim nationally and internationally. We would like to point out that Judaism has had pioneering work of its own to do as the Jewish people lived through the Holocaust and have come to understandings of where their God was in the profound pain and suffering of the community. It was a very tender moment for two Christian editors to read her chapter and to see and feel the powerful faith of the Jewish community that survived to sing songs of praises to a God who is there to hear their prayers for the dead.

PART III: OPENING THE ANCIENT TREASURE BOX OF FAITH

Professor Pinsky finds that, given her status as a third-wave feminist, it is difficult (as a younger feminist researcher) even to ask questions related to faith, believing, and belonging of the older feminist cohort that struggled through the culture wars of the 1960s. She feels that she and her generation benefitted by the earlier generations' struggles for egalitarian communities, by their innovation, questioning, and debate.

Professors Morgenstern, Erickson, and Karam belong to Jewish, Christian, and Islamic communities of faith; all three find the future of peaceable world communities to be anchored in the ability to ask critical questions and receive responsible answers. While it is true that the methodologies for building accountable relationships are rooted in faith traditions and respective knowledge bases, these professors have demonstrated that their university educations have much to offer these traditions in the way of methodological, practical, and theoretical insight, just as they offer these same insights and competent disciplinary contributions to their secular classrooms and professional institutions. All three have found resistance from the academic and/or social action arenas to their integration of the life worlds; because they know this integration to be necessary to the understanding of the critical issues facing a globalizing world culture, they have persisted.

Karam, a Muslim, believes that she is reclaiming her faith as she uses her academic and practical skills to understand further the politicization of religion. Erickson and Morgenstern find, along with Karam, that, just as Islam has formed complex moral communities over the centuries, so too have Christianity and Judaism. The task of university-trained scholars is to exegete these religio-cultural systems and work within the multiple levels of sociopolitical realities to bring about constructive growth. There are different strategies for accomplishing these goals. Karam brought her academic gifts to the

World Conference of Religions for Peace; Morgenstern and Erickson maintained academic posts while active in religious organizations.

Professor Susan Farrell writes a summary chapter demonstrating that one life may hold the range of experiences documented throughout the book. Her solid track record as a scholar and contributor to professional associations and her social-action agenda to transform her religious tradition find her making a well-stated case for moving feminist academic and social agendas away from the margins of society and church to the center. This is not always easy to do, as the academy is not always welcoming to those who openly profess or discuss matters of faith. In the discipline of sociology, the belief in the disenchantment and further rationalization of the social world that relegates religion to the private sphere makes personal discussions of religion somewhat difficult, if not downright discouraged. When Farrell put forward her thesis proposal, one member of her committee questioned the relevance of studying women in the Roman Catholic Church. After all, she asked, wouldn't the women simply leave once they had come to their senses? Farrell found that the women she studied were not leaving their church; they were out to revolutionize it.

On the other hand, she and many of her colleagues and co-workers find it difficult to belong to a church that does not support the advancement and liberation of women. Her continued faith keeps her engaged with the church as an institution. However, even that faith, as we heard so articulately from Lorber and Pinsky, is challenged by the sins against women, past and present. The real challenge to the feminist community, as for other kinds of social subgroups, is whether or not it is possible to hold on to the hope the tradition offers and therefore to feminists' sense of belonging to, their membership in, faith communities.

Hope is perhaps the most striking feature of these chapters. From biologist Temple's search for immunological cures to social activist Ammat'ullah's search to end racial and religio-cultural discrimination, from pioneer Lorber's search for comfort to Morgenstern's search to provide comfort to the seeking, we find hope to be the catalyst for change, for doing whatever we need to do to become more divinely human.

TOGETHER, WHO ARE WE?

If we look through the Ursuline Sisters' experience, learning, and identity lens (Chapter 9), we see that there is a continual cycling of these; our identity changes when experiences come to us and we learn anew who we are, what happened to us, and where we want life to go next. This book is a snapshot of our experiences, learning, and identity, frozen in time; yet on these pages we are able to see, hear, and feel these dynamic lives. What did these academics teach us? Why do they do what they do? What does their sharing of their life stories mean for the living of our lives?

IDENTITY

Our authors identify themselves in many ways: by religious faith traditions, ethnicity, gender, marital status, academic disciplines, spiritual awareness, professional responsibilities, theological awareness, generational placement in family, geography of origin—the state they grew up in, the region of the world they are from, the local community—and their status in the many communities in which they hold membership. We might consider these positive identity attributes.

However, they also identity themselves historically and contemporarily by negative elements—as a person and a member of a community that has been hurt in some way. The range of pain and suffering varies from chapter to chapter, but it is clear that all of our authors have experienced some kind of alienation from human community or individuals in it. A few of our authors have experienced real danger and will continue to live in the tricky and sticky areas of human rights, where life is lived on the edge.

Believing and belonging, or at least one of these, helped our authors survive the bad times, appreciate the good times, and plan for a more rewarding future for the next generation. What is compelling about their stories are the truths they live—they are all seeking to be the best they can be, to be authentically and divinely human.

EXPERIENCE

For most of our authors the level of resolve to change the negative aspects of life—racial, ethnic, gender, religious, and cultural discrimination—is remarkably anchored in historical memories and everyday understandings of God as just and loving. To a one, they believe that alienation is not necessary. The creating of the "other" as a person "not like me" is not necessary. There are peaceful and just alternatives to acts of domination and exclusion. Despite stories of suffering themselves, or with others, our authors remain optimistic lovers of people. They do not allow their anger to control their actions in a broken world; rather, anger becomes the energy they use to repair the world through right and good actions. The problem in human life is that we are always at some time or another in a stage of broken-heartedness. So we know, then, the difference between our suffering and our love, that transcendent force that corrects the lack of other relatedness when things go wrong and cause suffering. Actions that help to repair our suffering souls are the enjoyment of one another and our shared participation in music and the arts. Beauty in all forms restores and refreshes the soul.

A soul restored through prayer, worship, and meditation is a determined soul. Determined not to limit the power of God, determined to fulfill commitments to others, determined to help end the humiliation of self and others. This soul is equipped by education to bring about democratic relationships, unity in complex human environments, and choices for the next generation.

LEARNING

For most of our authors the sacred texts provide a foundation, resource, or guiding light for the changes they want to see in self and society. In the texts they find their stories of humiliation and alienation met by a loving God who defends them against injustice. In the texts and in historical memory the polarization and politicization of their lives are countered by stories of their people's courage and survival. Several of our authors see the future survival of the world as one in which religion helps to teach society how to make connections with others and how to transmit core values to our children. Most of our authors see their academic and spiritual vocations not only as divine handicraft but as products of a community, or of several communities, that created them and nurtured them into being accepting, open, and adventuresome people.

We feel compelled, called, to our work and our communities. There is something "otherworldly" or "beyond us" about our understanding of ourselves in context. However, scientists that we are, the editors can't resist categorizing what we read on these pages. Our authors fit an identity and action pattern that they themselves may be surprised to discover. They are all somewhere on a continuum of "commitment to religious thinking" that ends, should we choose to go there, at a community designation wherein we are named by others as "a major religious thinker." Professor Erickson taught a seminar called "Major Religious Thinkers" whose students produced the descriptions below after reading people such as the Hebrew heroes of faith, Jesus, Buddha, Rumi, Martin Luther, and Gandhi. Taking into account that our authors have not expressed any interest in becoming or being major religious thinkers, preferring to live authentic yet simple lives, what do you see in our professors' stories? Where do they fit into our students' reading and understanding of significant religious thinking? Where would Moses, Ruth, Jeremiah, Mary, Martha, or Timothy fit into this framework? Does it help to contrast our humble professors with people gone before them? Yes. When we do, we discover how very much our heroes in faith are like us—they all thought God was rather mistaken by choosing some one so simple and humble to do great things. God just smiled and sent them off toward the horizon.

Students' Summaries: Major Religious Thinkers and Thinking

- The world is one world for major religious thinkers. Religion, culture, and society are one reality. Religion's aim is to create an integrated world wherein both of the spiritual and social realities formed out of the interactions of bodies, souls, and minds, are accountable to Being/God/the Holy Other. Of equal importance to them is the human to human accountability of nonbelievers. The believer is accountable to others when he or she is accountable to God/the divine.
- Major religious thinkers use common ordinary occasions to assist people in shaping their spiritual, religious, and moral lives. Frequently, moving

toward the good life that is accountable to God requires changing human society, culture, and interpersonal actions. This change is often rooted in an examination of the people's story. Major religious thinkers help the people understand their role in constructing ordinary events and challenge them to restructure relationships in such a way as to accomplish the world they desire.

- The people's story is holy. In order to examine the actions that necessitate change (caused often by the wrongdoing of the people), major religious thinkers are careful to help people provide a social commentary that moves them toward the story's salvation. The eternal truths known to the people are held up as accomplishable by the whole. Through educational processes (for example, teachings, sermons, lectures or speeches, prayer, and meditations) the people are empowered to act courageously and, in so doing, pass on their values to the young.

- The empowerment of the people is accomplished through a deep love for them that creates positive and mass identification with anchoring values that encourage them to reach for still higher levels of oneness and solidarity. Major religious thinkers teach us how to live lives of peace, justice, and wholeness in a complex world.

Students' List of Attributes of Major Religious Thinkers

1. Understands the people.
2. Understands God in the lives of the people.
3. Is able to describe the people's experience clearly.
4. Describes the people's story so that they love the story, even though some of the characters fail.
5. Accepts the stranger, the outsider.
6. Narrates from a larger perspective than most of the people hold—has a global viewpoint and is able to enlarge the framework in order to help people understand their lives/their stories.
7. Overlooks the social norms, sees something above them—something to reach for—while keeping and working to change the law.
8. Does not engage or accept victim identities for self or others; promotes agency and courageous action.
9. Moves the story toward the story's salvation.
10. Helps the people provide social commentary.
11. Is unbiased in favoring or not favoring characters in the story—everybody is judged in the same way.
12. Uses educational tools that enhance religious thought, creating significant thoughts that change people and their way of life.
13. Has a positive attitude.
14. Provides accurate understandings of the situation from many points of view.
15. Seeks simplicity so that each reader, listener, actor, can see and understand.

16. Uses abstraction with reasoning that people can hear and follow, for example, telling parables.

17. Creates relevancy in the story promoting group-mass identification, solidarity.

18. Uses symbols or metaphors to increase understanding.

19. Lives by example.

20. Has a story and personality that people can relate to.

21. Expresses eternal truths.

22. Submits to God/Divine in an evident way.

23. Presents tradition that can be passed on to the people.

24. Provides a religious outlook that helps the religious community establish itself.

25. Moves and changes us.

26. Makes a contribution others did not make to our lives.

27. Translates texts (wisdom information) into the common person's vernacular.

28. Creates work and makes contributions that remain relevant across time.

29. Are well-educated or well-trained by the faith community, even if they never attended a formal school or are not known as "literate"; (however, they are increasingly formally educated and thought to be the highest wisdom source around).

The editors believe that our authors (all of them surprised when we asked them to write for us) did indeed produce significant religious thinking because they are spiritual people as well as significant moral actors in a variety of troubled contexts. A couple of our authors may not even think of themselves as religious thinkers at all. How surprised our authors must be when they look at our students' definitions and see themselves as rather accomplished. Whether or not the authors are or go on to become major religious thinkers is a matter best left to the judgment of others.

WHY DO WE DO WHAT WE DO?

RELIGIOUS THINKERS DO WHAT RELIGIOUS THINKERS DO!

It is perhaps important for us here to establish how one develops a nurturing, effective, and powerful spiritual life. To help us do this, we offer to our collective thinking the spiritual life of the Rev. Dr. Dietrich Bonhoeffer (1906–45) and the life-giving soul-companionship of Rabbi Dr. Abraham Joshua Heschel (1907–72) and the Rev. Dr. Martin Luther King Jr. (1929–68). Bonhoeffer's religious commitments cost him his life in an effort to halt Adolf Hitler's Holocaust horrors (see Kelly and Nelson 2003). Heschel and King met in January 1963. Ten days after he spoke to the Conservative Rabbis of America, who had gathered to celebrate Heschel's sixtieth birthday, King lost his life to an assassin in an effort to halt racism and its effects in the United States (see King 1990; Heschel 1997).

Pastor Dietrich Bonhoeffer understood that evil ideologies, when combined with immoral leadership, are capable of marching people to evil ends; therefore, it was important for him not only to organize a resistance movement against Hitler but to establish a theological, sociological, and political understanding of resistance, of right action. Why is right action holy and good? How close can we get people to this goal? Eventually our children and our children's children will want to know why we did what we did, so we should know this ourselves. What kind of spiritual life produced Bonhoeffer and his confessing community of Christians who expressed their spirituality in terms of personal and public morality as they sought to change both church and society?

WE SAY, "YES"

Bonhoeffer and companions said yes to God, the commandments of God, and to the needs of others. It was through prayer that they understood that their action to halt Hitler's regime was necessary. For this seemingly impossible effort they needed courage and a peaceable heart ready to forgive the wrongdoer but to hold the evildoer accountable for wrong actions. The *yes* to God obligates one to oppose evil; this obligation is the heart of orthopraxis, right action. Oriented rightly to God, Bonhoeffer's spirituality was oriented to moral leadership. The resistance movement's relationship with God, the church, and Jews was a spiritual one, one not just about resisting wickedness but about care-taking and the sharing of suffering and joy. Spirituality as response to God and the world provided those around the resistance movement with hope, encouragement, courage, and inspiration. When asked, "Who am I?" Bonhoeffer's reply was, "I am yours in life and death."

WE SAY, "I AM YOURS"

Bonhoeffer ended the duality, the dichotomy, between faith and political life. Faith was about solidarity with God and the people of God. Fidelity, compassion, wisdom, conviction, and true patriotism expanded his spirituality into a landscape big enough to hold us all. Christians were called to conform to the *pathos* of God, to end their silence, and to act. Bonhoeffer called on people, asking them to turn on the light. Of God, Bonhoeffer wrote:

> "The truth shall set you free." Not our courage, our strength, our people, our truth, but God's truth alone. To be free does not mean to be great in the world, to be free against our brothers and sisters, to be free against God; but it means to be free from ourselves, from our untruth. . . .

The people who love, because they are freed through the truth of God, are the most revolutionary people on earth. (Kelly and Nelson 2003, 83)

They are the people who love to use their gifts and talents to give life to others.

A refugee from Hitler's Europe, Rabbi Dr. Heschel had a love for the suffering and a passion for truth that sent him into an alliance with Rev. Dr. King Jr. Friends and co-workers in the vineyard of racial reconciliation, they both demonstrated a moral grandeur and a spiritual audacity that have come to characterize those who have no fear in the face of evil. From Seoul to New York City friends have worked hard to make sure these names stay linked. There was something divine and complete about these two men who bore prophetic witness to the power of soul speech. The language of the soul is piety itself. King and Heschel understood that what we say, what we pray for, and what we do with our bodies matters.

Susannah Heschel, the rabbi's daughter, claims that the real bonds between Heschel and King were theological ones built on spiritual connections linked to shared understandings of the Bible. Both believed that God was profoundly concerned with the suffering of black men and women in the United States and that God's pain was their pain too. Both were prophetic figures who said yes to each other, a relationship that became indelible in the mind of the world through the photograph of them marching together in Selma in March 1965. Although the Jewish community recognized Heschel's moral stature in his ability to chastise Jews for their racism, few Christians have adequately thanked him, or his memory, for his ability to chastise them in such a way that they knew he was right and that he loved them. For the Christian generations there was no greater sign of Heschel's profound disappointment with us than his need to show up and stand next to a Baptist minister in Selma. When Christians were not flooding in to support King, Heschel's prophetic moral imperative to stand for social justice modeled a living God whose judgment was leveled against the racism held by Jews and Christians.

King was awarded the Nobel Peace Prize for his work, but he knew that his faith and work were made possible by the commitment to justice and action of people like Heschel. It was simply the truth that these leaders believed that God wanted equality for all people. For them, there was no higher calling than the search for just living. This search found them hosting one dinner after the next. It is through table-talk that people come to understand each other. It is only through understanding that we have any hope of love. King and Heschel understood that people are converted to justice by the power of love.

WE ARE THERE IN LOVE

Regardless of where they are on the believing and belonging continuum, in simple, direct ways both big and small our authors are there for people when they are needed. They go to extraordinary places over extraordinary distances with their students. We call this love. The gift of a university education allows us to be there, meeting the needs of people, in special ways. But these ways are no more extraordinary than the pure gift of authenticity offered between two homeless people sitting on a park bench. After World War II ended, Bonhoeffer's confessing-community spirit spread into the Christian world and now feeds our efforts to help the poor and disenfranchised in American rural areas and inner cities, Latin America, Asia, Africa, and the Middle East.

What we learned in this book is that regardless of one's tradition in the Abrahamic family of Judaism, Christianity, and Islam, we are all commanded to work together charitably to end suffering and to teach one another new ways to love humanity. One group is not to consider itself superior to any other by virtue of book learning or literacy. We are all created by God to fulfill the law of love.

WE SET THE TABLE

Academics, as all people, must be responsible for the gifts we have been given. We are able to bring particular insights to the table of discussion, inquiry, and resolution. Irreducible among them is free speech. The table, classroom, or laboratory is the place to talk, to make mistakes, to bumble about, and eventually to come up with fine ideas. Free speech, then, leads to free thinking. Love-based speech and thinking creates theory and innovation that is good for people. What we have heard in these chapters is an insistence on the right to speak, even a "retaking of speech" in a speaking "in their own name," a being heard, "a making of history" (De Certeau 1997, 31). But this speech is not cut off from the people and the created world around them. Rather, these academics who believe and/or belong all see the importance of tradition (our long history), generations (the passing on of respect and care taking), and conjunctions (the "glue" of personal inventions that make society possible) (De Certeau 1997, viii).

In this sense, then, some places in the academy have some work to do to return to the academy's heritage of listening to tradition, respecting the accumulation of wisdom of its scholars, and making possible free thought for its future students. Whenever insight is cut off, whenever the light is turned off, whenever thinking and speaking are limited by ideology, the academy ceases to be the academy, because it ceases to be fed by human values. The limiting of the free voice seeking to be heard, nurtured, and given to the world for its salvation ultimately acts to throw the university itself into disrepair and decay. Scholars of faith know this. The university is the daughter of the church, synagogue, and mosque. She has struggled against both the ecclesiastical authorities and the police for the right to speak her truth. To limit the sources of truth she draws from is to re-create her as something she is not. Rather, what we see in this book is the flowering of science in the lives of scholars who are brave enough to live integrated lives in the many contexts in which they live and work. The rose of science is offered back to the faith community in the form of expanded, changed, and nurturing practices that seek more than survival, that seek to move the world toward peace and wholeness, toward its salvation. When scholars form a true *ummah* it becomes a refuge for the exhausted, a kind of human paradise in this world, a soul-place for real being.

TOWARD AN ABRAHAMIC SCHOLASTIC COMMUNITY: NEIGHBORLINESS, CHARITY, AND REPAIRING THE WORLD

We recommend to you Seyyed Hossein Nasr's *The Heart of Islam*. A successful scholarly effort to put academic knowledge into the average person's vernacular, *The Heart of Islam*, impresses several truths for the whole Abrahamic family. Startlingly true is this assessment:

> In the Quran God refers to Himself as al-Salam, or Peace, so that one could, as a Muslim, say that God is Peace and our yearning for peace is nothing more than our yearning for God. Deep down in our primordial nature there is still the recollection of the peace we experienced when we bore witness to God's Lordship in pre-eternity before our fall into this world of forgetfulness. . . . We still recall now and then that peace that Christ said "passeth all understanding." (Nasr 2002, 219)

Our forgetfulness causes profound problems for us. That is why we need scholars and laity who help us remember not only the basics of our faith but also that which is still to be born in us—the peace of God that is still to be ours on this earth. As the world globalizes and we come into increasing contact with one another, remembering helps us maintain a steady course on the rough seas of life. Professor Nasr writes of religious scholars: "These scholars and leaders seek to preserve the rhythm of traditional Islamic life as well as its intellectual and spiritual traditions and find natural allies in Judaism and Christianity in confronting the challenges of modern secularism and globalization" (Nasr 2002, 108). Life has always been better for us when we help one another, study together, pray for one another's well-being, and share the simple joys of life. We need to remember this.

Inside of the Islamic *ummah* religious and spiritual innovation, new interpretations of the text, and new directions are studied as a consensus is formed regarding the sense these make in light of history and tradition. Keeping everyone on the *straight path* is the goal of consensus. All three traditions seek to know God, to become compassionate and responsible members of the world community. We might wonder, then, why it is that we spend so little time reasoning together? If the goal of our God is one community, why do we maintain fragmented lives? The quick answer always seems to be, "If we reason together, are we then abandoning our own truth?" Afraid to find out, thinking that we will lose something and not gain anything, we stay too far away from one another. Of course, if we use our coming together as occasions to convert the "other" to our way of thinking, we will never reason together—and we will push one another still further away. We need to remember those times in our shared histories when the Abrahamic family supported one another, got along well, and established a university life that was the envy of the world. It was out of our shared life that we produced the university at Cordova. It was out of stellar conversations with Muslims that our much celebrated Jewish scholar Moses Maimonides arose. There is still in us a memory of how to talk with one another, how to understand one another, how to live with one another. The way back to the good times might be through everyday events such as shared meals, dancing, and shared acts of charity.

What we have learned from our Muslim colleagues is that *charity* is a much larger concept and practice than the modern West understands when it hears the word. Charity to the average American brings up images of stuffing a dollar bill into a Salvation Army box as some cold soul is ringing a bell, trying to focus our attention on the needs of others. Most Muslims I know see the bigger picture. They see the dedicated lives of the Salvation Army members, the neighborhood programs, their national and international relief efforts. That's charity. The giving of one's self to the well-being of the world includes the giving of intellectual and physical resources, and yes, money. This is also something else, something the Jewish community calls *tikkun olum* (repairing the world).

Repairing the world is an act of justice in the Jewish tradition, as charity is in Islam. In all three traditions we call this charitable repair work *healing*. It is good to remember that righteousness and justice are the foundation of God's safeguarding order. The Sages wrote, extolling Psalm 68:5, that the protection of the defenseless is God's holy dwelling, God's *araboth*. As Maimonides says, "*Araboth*—that in which exist righteousness, right-dealing, justice, the treasures of life, the treasures of peace, the treasures of blessing, the soul of the righteous ones, the souls and the spirits that shall be created in the future" (Pines 1963, 173–74). Our very origin comes from the *araboth* of God.

READING OUR HOLY BOOKS:
TOGETHER UNDERSTANDING
AND PRODUCING HOLY PEACE AND JUSTICE

A teacher invited her students to name their communities' values in their papers; most often it was her Muslim students who would cite their holy book, the Qur'an. She remembers one socio-economic paper that presented two models for world (global) economics. One was a summary of the current Western model, and the other was a summary of what world economics would be like if economical life held the values of the Qur'an. The result seemed like paradise in the ways that even Jews and Christians would describe a just and peaceful world. Over the course of the semester the class discussed, and the students wrote more papers on, the realities of a diverse world and how we might integrate the many values systems that make the United States home to immigrants from all over the world—and indeed, how we as a world could integrate our many peoples on a global level while maintaining the diversity that makes us great and that we call divine handicraft.

What impressed the teacher most over the years was the Muslim students' understanding that their faith was the source of peace; it led her into deeper readings of Muslim theologians, philosophers, religionists, jurists, physicists, and many more. Students know that the power of believing is anchored in a real, historical, and ongoing community of faith, its hope and vision. Central to Muslim life is the Qur'an.

It is time in America for Christians and Jews to understand the Qur'an, and it is time for Muslims to hear Jews and Christians explain the living hope and vision anchored in their ancient texts, in conversations across time, and in current realities. As this Christian reads the Qur'an, she finds believers in Allah submitting to the divine truth, to Allah, and therein receiving forgiveness and salvation (Surah 3.16, 52). The prophets are, every one, cherished for their insight (Surah 3.84). The Beneficent God (Surah 67.29) is the foundation of a just world, a world brought about by many things, but surely also by the believers' remembering that God "will see your doings, then you shall be brought back to the Knower of the unseen and the seen, then He will inform you of what you did" (Surah 9.94).

To help us do good things, the Qur'an asks Muslims to have believers for friends and to be "the best" of the nations raised up for mankind, enjoining what is right and forbidding what is wrong, and believing in Allah (Surah 3.110). The all-hearing and all-knowing Allah asks believers to be like Allah, with compassion for everyone, providing safety (Surah 5.16; 9.6) and protection (2.286; 4.96). Humbling ourselves, we are to extend to orphans, the needy, our neighbors, our kins' neighbors, and neighbors we do not know, including the wayfarer met on a journey, our very goodness as Allah is good (Surah 4.36).

Doing goodness is the foundation for a just world, a world the Muslim students in the class knew was possible. This just world starts with prayer and moves into the home and into society (Surah 7.29). Taking the high road, the straight path to God, Muslims become peacemakers and not mischief makers (Surah 2.11). So precious is a just peace to Allah that we hear the greeting "peace be upon you" as a special blessing from the servants of God. Reading the Qur'an, praying, and listening to other believers who seek peace are the first steps toward the world we know is possible. Precious to God is our continued study and our care taking of the earth.

Muslim students are often amused to hear Christian and Jewish students talking as if they do not know each other—and they don't really. To Muslims, Christians and Jews are Peoples of the Book, people of a kind. The gentle teasing of Muslim students has created surprise in Christians and Jews who have developed surprising closeness through their Muslim friends' reflections. The Qur'an tells Muslims to do what they can to improve the spiritual lives of non-Muslims. Society teaches Christians and Jews that they have little in common. Of course, many Christians and Jews have come to know each other well, but this is often after meeting in adulthood for the first time in colleges and other social institutions. It is in schools that all three—Muslims, Christians, and Jews—come to meet one another in significant ways. It is often through the chaplain's office that serious conversations happen between the groups, but we forget that the classroom is the most common meeting ground. Members of the Abrahamic family have a lot in common; all three listen closely to the others in the classroom.

In common, we value among the believers the time we share in fellowship, what Christians call "the breaking of the bread" (Acts 2:42). Jews and Christians, like Muslims, value prayer and the company of other believers. Yet this closeness is not to prevent believers from seeing the needs of others, giving charity to them, and protecting the strangers as if they were angels (Ex 22:21; 23:9; Lv 25; Matt 23:35; Heb 13:2; 3 Jn 1:5). Christians might learn a lot from the Muslim reading of their historic relationship to Jews. Christians inherit their important and foundational understanding of neighbor from Judaism. We are taught to share food with our neighbors (Ex 12), not to speak falsely about them or covet their possessions (Ex 20). Being fair to one's neighbor (Ex 19) also requires speaking the truth to the neighbor (Lv 19; Prov 3:28–30). This good treatment of neighbors does not mean that one should let one's family be taken advantage of by "bad" neighbors, but it does point to a central truth in human relationships—when we treat people kindly, they are more apt to be kind themselves. From Judaism, Christians learn through Jesus that we are to love our neighbors, friends, and enemies (Matt 5:42–44). We are to love our neighbors as ourselves (Matt 22:38–40). Everyone near and far is our neighbor, the person we have met and the person we have not yet met; we are to love this person and in so doing, realize that when we love, we have fulfilled the law (Rom 13:9–11). When we love our neighbor, we do right (Jas 2:8; Lv 19:18).

Doing right is the heart of justice. We are told not to side with the crowd in its wrongdoing (Ex 23), show favoritism to the great (Lv 19:14–16), or withhold justice from the defenseless (Dt 27). The governing of the people is difficult enough, so the psalms tell us not to plot injustice (Ps 58) and to act like the royal children of God, judging people with righteousness while acting justly ourselves. We are not to mock people or create instability (Prov 19). When we learn to do right and then do it, the oppressed are encouraged (Isa 1:17) and the people anticipate redemption. When we act justly, God is exalted and the people have hope (Isa 5:15–17). For Jews and Christians, there are perhaps no better known verses regarding justice than "let justice roll on like a river, righteousness like a never-failing stream!" (Am 5:24) and "what does the Lord require of you? To act justly, and to love mercy and to walk humbly with your God" (Mi 6:8). Justice is brought about by people we call peacemakers. In fact we do more than that; we say with Jesus, "Blessed are the peacemakers, for they will be called children of God" (Matt 5:9).

A GOOD TIME FOR US

Our framework for this book has been a sociological one. Both editors are sociologists, educated together at the City University of New York Graduate Center. In fact, we discussed this project over several years of continued friendship. We believe and see the world, as our individual essays make clear, through a sociological lens, as well as through our respective faith traditions. We have also both had theological training. But we used the "sociological imagination" to think about believing, belonging, and living the faith on the margins of religious institutions. This imagination, envisioning, encourages us to see the interconnectedness of our worlds and their traditions, to see how individual lives are connected with larger social issues (for the classic source of this insight, see Mills 1959). Other authors in this book have used other disciplinary analyses and frameworks to examine their lives. What we all share is the desire to do the analyses and find the connections, the correlations, the ways in which our faith traditions have sustained us in our academic and professional lives, albeit not always easily or without conflict. These analyses also help us to see the connections with one another and with the larger world and its problems: war, imperialism, neocolonialism, militarism, and, from a sociological perspective, what may be at the root of many of these problems: ethnocentrism or egocentrism, any narrowing and favoring of one subset of humanity. Yet, we all find hope within these religious traditions—a hope that may bring us closer in our conversation together.

The interesting thing about hope is that it does not need an imagination, as in the statement "hope springs eternal." Amitai Etzioni and David E. Carney's sociological and interdisciplinary examination of repentance makes clear that our hope is founded on a moral life that assumes that people will regret their sins, be determined not to repeat them and seek forgiveness. The absence of these human values is hard to imagine (see Neusner 1997). Human society is continually changing and adapting as it moves toward the unity that is our hope. The path to this unity is what requires our imagination. How do we in the United States become an increasingly global culture? What is religion's role (that is, what is religion up to and what is it doing?) in helping us retain core values as we change so that the peaceful, just, and unified society we want materializes?

In an article reporting on their study of immigrant religiosity, F. Yang and H. Ebaugh find that new Americans tend to gravitate toward a cultural style of congregational ritual and organizational life, that they return to theological thinking, and that they include others in building a new life in America (see Yang and Ebaugh 2001). The expansion of lay leadership is a common experience among the religious traditions of new Americans; as they communicate back home, this transformation of religious experience is put into dialogue with the world community.

The diversity of ethnic populations in metropolitan areas automatically creates a sense of wonder and curiosity as neighbors walk in through the doors of religious houses. This cross-cultural contact is good for immigrant groups that find themselves explaining their traditions and, in so doing, expanding knowledge about them. Our problems are not related to what is good but to what is bad about our encounters with one another. Violent clashes are results of profound disconnections that transgress resident values. What we need in the West are expanded opportunities to share our life worlds and to discover our values. Out of these opportunities we will form friendships and working relationships that build a shared future.

Our authors' stories support studies done in Jerusalem and Amsterdam that found significant correlations in the values that adherents to various religions (Israeli Jews, Spanish Catholics, Dutch Calvinist Protestants, and Greek Orthodox) favor and disfavor (see Schwartz and Huismans 1995). The religious traditions under study favored universalism (world peace, beauty, and broad-mindedness), benevolence, tradition, conformity, and security. Disfavoring hedonism and self-direction, religious traditions moved toward cooperation that brings about security for family and nation. Values favoring restraint and submission to superior truths characterize the religious. Given the value statements we have read in these chapters, it would seem, then, that now is a good time for women scholars and their students to join and to form national and international agendas for scientific and religious Abrahamic family conversations. And, in the spirit of Rochelle Garner's *Contesting the Terrain of the Ivory Tower* (2004), take the risk of naming leaders and leadership styles that are no longer worthy of public trust, and ultimately of replacing them with empowered leaders who become agents of hope, love, confidence, respect, dignity, harmony, ambition, responsibility, and the courage to change.

Reference List

Bach, Alice, ed. 1999. *Women in the Hebrew Bible*. New York: Routledge.

Bakhtin, Mikhail Mikhalovich. 1981. *The Dialogic Imagination*. Edited by M. Holquist. Austin: Univ. of Texas Press.

Ball-Rokeach, Sandra J. 1973. "From Pervasive Ambiguity to a Definition of the Situation." *Sociometry* 36/3: 378–89.

Barlas, Asma. 2002. *Believing Women in Islam*. Austin, TX: Texas Univ. Press.

Christ, Carol, and Judith Plaskow, eds. 1979. *Womanspirit Rising: A Feminist Reader in Religion*. San Francisico: Harper & Row.

Cohen, Steven M., and Arnold M. Eisen. 2000. *The Jew Within: Self, Family, and Community in America*. Bloomington: Indiana Univ. Press.

Collins, Randall. 1986. "The Passing of Intellectual Generations: Reflections on the Death of Erving Goffman." *Sociological Theory* 4: 106–13.

Cromer, Alan. 1993. *Uncommon Sense: The Heretical Nature of Science*. New York: Oxford Univ. Press.

Dahan-Kalev, Henriette. 2001. "Tensions in Israeli Feminism: The Mizrahi-Ashkenazi Rift." *Women Studies International Forum* 24.

Davidman, Lynn. 1991. *Tradition in a Rootless World: Women Turn to Orthodox Judaism*. Berkeley and Los Angeles: Univ. of California Press.

De Certeau, Michel. 1997. *The Capture of Speech*. Translated by T. Conley. Minneapolis: Univ. of Minnesota Press.

Douglas, Mary. 1992. "The Debate on Women Priests." In *Risk and Blame: Essays in Cultural Theory*. New York: Routledge.

Erickson, Victoria Lee. 1993. *Where Silence Speaks*. Minneapolis: Fortress Press.

———. 1999. "Society Is an Act of Faith." *The Living Pulpit* 8/3 (July-September).

———. 2001. "Georg Simmel: American Sociology Chooses the Stone the Builder Rejected." In *Blackwell Companion to the Sociology of Religion*, edited by Richard K. Fenn. Oxford: Blackwell.

———. 2002. "Social Theory and Sacred Text and Sing Sing Prison." In *Religion, the Community and the Rehabilitation of Criminal Offenders*, edited by Thomas P. O'Conner and Nathaniel J. Pallone. Binghamton, NY: Haworth Press.

———. 2003. "Faith Communities" and "Healing." In *Encyclopedia of Community*, directed by Karen Christensen. Berkshire Publishing Group.

Erikson, Erik. 1963. *Childhood and Society*. New York: W. W. Norton and Co.

Fabel, Arthur, and Donald St. John. 2003. *Teilhard and the Twenty-first Century*. Maryknoll, NY: Orbis Books.

Feiner, Shmuel. 1996. "The Pseudo-Enlightenment and the Question of Jewish Modernization." *Jewish Social Studies* 3: 62–88.

Fishman, Sylvia Barack. 1993. *A Breath of Life: Feminism in the American Jewish Community*. New York: Free Press.

Foucault, Michel. 1962. "Le 'non' du père." *Critique* 178 (March).

Frankel, Ellen. 1998. *The Five Books of Miriam*. San Francisco: HarperSanFrancisco.

Frymer-Kensky, Tikva, ed. 2002. *Reading the Women of the Bible.* New York: Schocken.

Gaarlandt, J. G., ed. 1985. *An Interrupted Life: The Diaries of Etty Hillesum 1941–43.* New York: Washington Square Press.

Ganss, George E. 1991. *Ignatius of Loyola: "Spiritual Exercises" and Selected Works.* New York: Paulist Press.

Garner, Rochelle. 2004. *Contesting the Terrain of the Ivory Tower: Spiritual Leadership of African-American Women in the Academy.* New York: Routledge.

Gillman, Neil. 1990. *Sacred Fragments: Recovering Theology for the Modern Jew.* Philadelphia: The Jewish Publication Society.

Goodenough, Ursula. 1998. *The Sacred Depths of Nature.* Oxford: Oxford Univ. Press.

Haan, Norma, et al. 1985. *On Moral Grounds.* New York: New York Univ. Press.

Haught, John. 2003. *Deeper Than Darwin.* Cambridge, MA: Westview Press.

Hauptman, Judith. 1998. *Rereading the Rabbis: A Woman's Voice.* Boulder, CO: Westview Press.

Hays, Sharon. 1994. "Structure and Agency and the Sticky Problem of Culture." *Sociological Theory* 12/1: 57–72.

Herzog, Hanna. 1999. "A Space of Their Own: Social-Civil Discourses among Palestinian-Israeli Women in Peace Organizations." *Social Politics: International Studies of Gender, State and Society* 6.

Heschel, Abraham Joshua. 1997. *Moral Grandeur and Spiritual Audacity: Essays by Abraham Joshua Heschel,* edited by Susannah Heschel. New York: Farrar, Straus and Giroux.

Hyman, Paula. 1995. *Gender and Assimilation in Modern Jewish History: The Roles and Representations of Women.* Seattle: Univ. of Washington Press.

Izraeli, Dafna Nundi. 2003. "Gender Politics in Israel: The Case of Affirmative Action for Women Directors." *Women's Studies International Forum* 26.

Johnson, Elizabeth. 1997. *She Who Is: The Mystery of God in Feminist Theological Discourse.* New York: Crossroad.

Johnson, Harriet McBryde. 2003. "Unspeakable Conversations." *New York Times Magazine* (February 16).

Karam, Azza. 1998a. *Islamisms and the State.* New York: Macmillan.

———. 1998b. *Women in Parliament: Beyond Numbers.* Stockholm: International IDEA.

———. 2004. *Transnational Political Islam.* Sterling, VA: Pluto Press.

Kates, Judith A., and Gail Twersky Reimer, eds. 1994. *Reading Ruth.* New York: Ballantine.

Kelly, G. B., and F. B. Nelson. 2003. *The Cost of Moral Leadership: The Spirituality of Dietrich Bonhoeffer.* Grand Rapids, MI: Eerdmans.

Kien, Jenny. 2000. *Reinstating the Divine Woman in Judaism.* Universal Publishers/uPublish.com.

King, Martin Luther, Jr. 1990. *A Testament of Hope: The Essential Writings and Speeches of Martin Luther King, Jr.,* edited by James M. Washington. San Francisco: HarperSanFrancisco.

Kingsolver, Barbara. 1998. *The Poisonwood Bible.* New York: Harper Collins.

Kittay, Eve. 1999. *Love's Labor.* New York: Routledge.

Kosmin, Barry A. 1991. *Highlights of the CJF 1990 National Jewish Population Survey.* New York: Council of Jewish Federations.

Lamm, Norman. 1999. *The Religious Thought of Hasidim*. New York: Yeshiva Univ. Press.

Lee, G. Avery. 1993. *Living in the Meantime*. Macon, GA: Smyth and Helwys.

Levin, Tobe. 2000. "Feminism: Jewish." In *Routledge International Encyclopedia of Women*, edited by Chries Kramara and Dale Spender, 2:774–80. New York: Routledge.

Levinas, Emmanuel. 1961. *Totality and Infinity*. Pittsburgh: Duquesne Univ. Press.

Lodhi, M. A. K., ed. 1989. *Islamization of Attitudes and Practices in Science and Technology*. Herndon, VA: International Institute of Islamic Thought.

Matt, Daniel C. 1996. *The Essential Kabbalah: The Heart of Jewish Mysticism*. New York: Harper Collins.

Matthews, D. A., et al. 2000. "The Efficacy of 'Distant Learning': A Systematic Review of Randomized Trials." *Annals of Internal Medicine*. June.

McDannell, Colleen. 1996. *Material Christianity: Religion and Popular Culture in America*. New Haven, CT: Yale Univ. Press.

Merton, Robert K. 1972. "Insiders and Outsiders: A Chapter in the Sociology of Knowledge." *American Journal of Sociology* 77 (July): 9–47.

Mills, C. Wright. 1959. *The Sociological Imagination*. New York: Oxford Univ. Press.

Morgenstern, Mira. 1999. "Ruth and the Sense of Self: Midrash and Difference." *Judaism*. (Spring).

———. 2000. "A Life in Code." In *Jewish Mothers Tell Their Stories: Acts of Love and Courage*, edited by Rachel Josefowitz Siegel, et al. Binghamton, NY: Haworth Press.

Nasr, Seyyed Hossein. 2002. *The Heart of Islam: Enduring Values for Humanity*. San Francisco: HarperSanFranciso.

Neusner, Jacob. 1997. "Repentance in Judaism." In *Repentance: A Comparative Perspective*. New York: Rowman & Littlefield.

Nussbaum, Martha. 1990. *Love's Knowledge*. New York: Oxford Univ. Press.

Patai, Raphael. 1990. *The Hebrew Goddess*. 3rd ed. Detroit, MI: Wayne State Univ. Press.

Pines, Shlomo, trans. 1963. Maimonides. *Guide of the Perplexed*. Chicago: Univ. of Chicago Press.

Pogrebin, Letty Cottin. 2003. "Attention Must Be Paid: How a Jewish Feminist Fought against Anti-Semitism in the Women's Movement." *Journey* (Spring).

Roemer, Michael. 1995. *Telling Stories*. Boston: Rowman & Littlefield.

Ruether, Rosemary Radford. 1975. *New Woman/New Earth: Sexist Strategies and Human Liberation*. New York: The Seabury Press.

Schwartz, S., and S. Huismans. 1995. "Values, Priorities, and Religiosity in Four Western Traditions." *Social Psychology Quarterly* 58/2: 88–107.

Silver, Mitchell. 1998. *Respecting the Wicked Child: A Philosophy of Secular Jewish Identity and Education*. Amherst: Univ. of Massachusetts Press.

Simmel, Georg. 1950. *The Sociology of Georg Simmel*. Translated by K. H. Wolff. Glencoe: Free Press.

———. 1997. *Essays on Religion*. Translated by H. Jurgen Helle. New Haven, CT: Yale Univ. Press.

Spain, Daphne. 2001. *How Women Saved the City*. Minneapolis: Univ. of Minnesota Press.

Starr, B. E. 1996. "The Tragedy of the Kingdom: Simmel and Troeltsch on Prophetic Religion." *The Journal of Religious Ethics* 24 (Spring): 141–67.

Swimme, Brian, and Thomas Berry. 1992. *The Universe Story: From the Primordial Flaring Forth to the Ecozoic Era: A Celebration of the Unfolding of the Cosmos*. San Francisco: Harper.

Teilhard de Chardin, Pierre. 1960. *The Divine Milieu*. New York. Harper & Row.

———. 1999. *The Human Phenomenon*. Translated by Susan Appleton-Weber. Portland, OR: Sussex Academic Press.

Van Leeuwen, M. S. 1990. *Gender and Grace: Love, Work, and Parenting in a Changing World*. Downers Grove, IL: Intervarsity Press.

Wade, Nicholas. 2003. "We Got Rhythm." *New York Times*. September 16.

Wadud, Amina. 1999. *Qur'an and Woman: Rereading the Sacred Text from a Woman's Perspective*. New York: Oxford Univ. Press.

Wertheimer, Jack. 1996. *Conservative Synagogues and Their Members: Highlights of the North American Survey of 1995–96*. New York: Jewish Theological Seminary of America.

Wieseltier, Leon. 2000. *Kaddish*. New York: Vintage.

Wuthnow, Robert. 1993. *Christianity in the Twenty-first Century*. New York: Oxford Univ. Press.

Yang, F., and H. Ebaugh. 2001. "Transformation in New Immigrant Religions and Their Global Implications." *American Sociological Review* 66/2: 269–88.

Young, Michael P. 2002. "Confessional Protest: The Religious Birth of U.S. National Social Movements." *American Sociological Review* 67: 660–88.

Other Titles in the Faith Meets Faith Series

Experiencing Scripture in World Religions, Harold Coward, Editor

The Meeting of Religions and the Trinity, Gavin D'Costa

Subverting Hatred: The Challenge of Nonviolence in Religious Traditions, Daniel L. Smith-Christopher, Editor

Christianity and Buddhism: A Multi-Cultural History of their Dialogue, Whalen Lai and Michael von Brück

Islam, Christianity, and the West: A Troubled History, Rollin Armour, Sr.

Many Mansions? Multiple Religious Belonging, Catherine Cornille, Editor

No God But God: A Path to Muslim-Christian Dialogue on the Nature of God, A. Christian van Gorder

Understanding Other Religious Worlds: A Guide for Interreligious Education, Judith Berling

Buddhists and Christians: Toward Solidarity through Comparative Theology, James L. Fredericks

Christophany: The Fullness of Man, Raimon Panikkar

Experiencing Buddhism: Ways of Wisdom and Compassion, Ruben L. F. Habito

Gandhi's Hope: Learning from Others as a Way to Peace, Jay B. McDaniel